The Essential Air Fryer Cookbook for Beginners UK

2000 Days Quick, Effortless and Flavorful Air Fryer Recipes for Healthier Frying Incl. Side Dishes, Desserts, Snacks and More

Damaris Gutkowski

Table of Contents

Chapter 3 Beef, Pork, and Lamb

Chapter 4 Fish and Seafood

Chapter 5 Poultry

Chapter 6 Vegetables and Sides

Chapter 7 Vegetarian Mains   47

Chapter 8 Desserts   53

Appendix 1 Measurement Conversion Chart   60

Appendix 2 Air Fryer Cooking Chart   61

INTRODUCTION

Air fryers have taken the culinary world by storm, providing a healthy and convenient alternative to deep-frying. This innovative kitchen appliance is capable of producing crispy, golden brown food with just a fraction of the oil needed in traditional frying methods. As a result, it's become a staple in many households, especially for those who are looking to maintain a healthier lifestyle.

An air fryer operates by circulating hot air around food, which results in the food being cooked evenly and crisply. The high-speed fan and hot air work together to cook food quickly and efficiently, which makes it an ideal appliance for busy families and individuals. Additionally, it's also much easier to clean than traditional deep fryers, making it a preferred choice for many people.

In this recipe book, we have put together a collection of delicious air fryer recipes that are easy to follow and produce delicious results. From appetizers to main dishes, and even desserts, you'll find something for every meal of the day. Whether you're a beginner or an experienced cook, you'll be able to make delicious meals with the help of this recipe book.

One of the great things about air frying is that it allows you to enjoy your favorite foods with less guilt. You can fry up chicken wings, mozzarella sticks, and French fries without the added calories and unhealthy oils. Additionally, air frying is also a great way to cook vegetables, making them crispy and delicious while retaining their nutrients.

Another advantage of air frying is that it's a great way to reduce food waste. Since the appliance is compact and takes up less space in your kitchen, you can easily store it away when not in use. This makes it an ideal choice for people who live in apartments or small homes.

So, whether you're looking to switch up your cooking routine, eat healthier, or simply want to try something new, this air fryer recipe book is for you. With simple and easy-to-follow recipes, you'll be able to create delicious meals in no time. So, let's get started and explore the world of air frying!

In conclusion, air fryers are an innovative and versatile kitchen appliance that provides a healthy and convenient way to fry food. With this recipe book, you'll have access to a collection of delicious recipes that you can make with ease. So, why wait? Get your air fryer ready and start

Chapter 1 Breakfasts

Easy Sausage Pizza

Prep time: 10 minutes | Cook time: 6 minutes | Serves 4

2 tablespoons ketchup

1 pitta bread

80 ml sausage meat

230 g Mozzarella cheese

1 teaspoon garlic powder

1 tablespoon olive oil

1. Preheat the air fryer to 172ºC. 2. Spread the ketchup over the pitta bread. 3. Top with the sausage meat and cheese. Sprinkle with the garlic powder and olive oil. 4. Put the pizza in the air fryer basket and bake for 6 minutes. 5. Serve warm.

Egg White Cups

Prep time: 10 minutes | Cook time: 15 minutes | Serves 4

475 ml 100% liquid egg whites

3 tablespoons salted butter, melted

¼ teaspoon salt

¼ teaspoon onion granules

½ medium plum tomato, cored and diced

120 ml chopped fresh spinach leaves

1. In a large bowl, whisk egg whites with butter, salt, and onion granules. Stir in tomato and spinach, then pour evenly into four ramekins greased with cooking spray. 2. Place ramekins into air fryer basket. Adjust the temperature to 150ºC and bake for 15 minutes. Eggs will be fully cooked and firm in the center when done. Serve warm.

Keto Quiche

Prep time: 10 minutes | Cook time: 1 hour | Makes 1 (6-inch) quiche

Crust:

300 ml blanched almond flour

300 ml grated Parmesan or Gouda cheese

¼ teaspoon fine sea salt

1 large egg, beaten

Filling:

120 ml chicken or beef stock (or vegetable stock for vegetarian)

235 ml shredded Swiss cheese (about 110 g)

110 g cream cheese (120 ml)

1 tablespoon unsalted butter, melted

4 large eggs, beaten

80 ml minced leeks or sliced spring onions

¾ teaspoon fine sea salt

⅛ teaspoon cayenne pepper

Chopped spring onions, for garnish

1. Preheat the air fryer to 164ºC. Grease a pie pan. Spray two large pieces of parchment paper with avocado oil and set them on the countertop. 2. Make the crust: In a medium-sized bowl, combine the flour, cheese, and salt and mix well. Add the egg and mix until the dough is well combined and stiff. 3. Place the dough in the center of one of the greased pieces of parchment. Top with the other piece of parchment. Using a rolling pin, roll out the dough into a circle about 1/16 inch thick. 4. Press the pie crust into the prepared pie pan. Place it in the air fryer and bake for 12 minutes, or until it starts to lightly brown. 5. While the crust bakes, make the filling: In a large bowl, combine the stock, Swiss cheese, cream cheese, and butter. Stir in the eggs, leeks, salt, and cayenne pepper. When the crust is ready, pour the mixture into the crust. 6. Place the quiche in the air fryer and bake for 15 minutes. Turn the heat down to 150ºC and bake for an additional 30 minutes, or until a knife inserted 1 inch from the edge comes out clean. You may have to cover the edges of the crust with foil to prevent burning. 7. Allow the quiche to cool for 10 minutes before garnishing it with chopped spring onions and cutting it into wedges. 8. Store leftovers in an airtight container in the refrigerator for up to 4 days or in the freezer for up to a month. Reheat in a preheated 176ºC air fryer for a few minutes, until warmed through.

Green Eggs and Ham

Prep time: 5 minutes | Cook time: 10 minutes | Serves 2

1 large Hass avocado, halved and pitted

2 thin slices ham

2 large eggs

2 tablespoons chopped spring onions, plus more for garnish

½ teaspoon fine sea salt

¼ teaspoon ground black pepper

60 ml shredded Cheddar cheese (omit for dairy-free)

1. Preheat the air fryer to 204ºC. 2. Place a slice of ham into the cavity of each avocado half. Crack an egg on top of the ham, then sprinkle on the green onions, salt, and pepper. 3. Place the avocado halves in the air fryer cut side up and air fry for 10 minutes, or until the egg is cooked to your desired doneness. Top with the cheese (if using) and air fry for 30 seconds more, or until the cheese is melted. Garnish with chopped green onions. 4. Best served fresh. Store extras in an airtight container in the fridge for up to 4 days. Reheat in a preheated 176ºC air fryer for a few minutes, until warmed through.

Egg in a Hole

Prep time: 5 minutes | Cook time: 5 minutes | Serves 1

1 slice bread
1 teaspoon butter, softened
1 egg
Salt and pepper, to taste

1 tablespoon shredded Cheddar cheese
2 teaspoons diced ham

1. Preheat the air fryer to 166ºC. Place a baking dish in the air fryer basket. 2. On a flat work surface, cut a hole in the center of the bread slice with a 2½-inch-diameter biscuit cutter. 3. Spread the butter evenly on each side of the bread slice and transfer to the baking dish. 4. Crack the egg into the hole and season as desired with salt and pepper. Scatter the shredded cheese and diced ham on top. 5. Bake in the preheated air fryer for 5 minutes until the bread is lightly browned and the egg is cooked to your preference. 6. Remove from the basket and serve hot.

Red Pepper and Feta Frittata

Prep time: 10 minutes | Cook time: 20 minutes | Serves 4

Olive oil cooking spray
8 large eggs
1 medium red pepper, diced
½ teaspoon salt

½ teaspoon black pepper
1 garlic clove, minced
120 ml feta, divided

1. Preheat the air fryer to 182ºC. Lightly coat the inside of a 6-inch round cake pan with olive oil cooking spray. 2. In a large bowl, beat the eggs for 1 to 2 minutes, or until well combined. 3. Add the red pepper, salt, black pepper, and garlic to the eggs, and mix together until the red pepper is distributed throughout. 4. Fold in 60 ml the feta cheese. 5. Pour the egg mixture into the prepared cake pan, and sprinkle the remaining 60 ml feta over the top. 6. Place into the air fryer and bake for 18 to 20 minutes, or until the eggs are set in the center. 7. Remove from the air fryer and allow to cool for 5 minutes before serving.

Spinach Omelet

Prep time: 5 minutes | Cook time: 12 minutes | Serves 2

4 large eggs
350 ml chopped fresh spinach leaves
2 tablespoons peeled and chopped brown onion

2 tablespoons salted butter, melted
120 ml shredded mild Cheddar cheese
¼ teaspoon salt

1. In an ungreased round nonstick baking dish, whisk eggs. Stir in spinach, onion, butter, Cheddar, and salt. 2. Place dish into air fryer basket. Adjust the temperature to 160ºC and bake for 12 minutes. Omelet will be done when browned on the top and firm in the middle. 3. Slice in half and serve warm on two medium plates.

Gyro Breakfast Patties with Tzatziki

Prep time: 10 minutes | Cook time: 20 minutes per batch | Makes 16

patties
Patties:
900 g lamb or beef mince
120 ml diced red onions
60 ml sliced black olives
2 tablespoons tomato sauce
1 teaspoon dried oregano leaves
2 cloves garlic, minced
1 teaspoon fine sea salt
Tzatziki:
235 ml full-fat sour cream
1 small cucumber, chopped

½ teaspoon fine sea salt
½ teaspoon garlic powder, or 1 clove garlic, minced
¼ teaspoon dried dill, or 1 teaspoon finely chopped fresh dill
For Garnish/Serving:
120 ml crumbled feta cheese (about 60 g)
Diced red onions
Sliced black olives
Sliced cucumbers

1. Preheat the air fryer to 176ºC. 2. Place the lamb, onions, olives, tomato sauce, oregano, garlic, and salt in a large bowl. Mix well to combine the ingredients. 3. Using your hands, form the mixture into sixteen 3-inch patties. Place about 5 of the patties in the air fryer and air fry for 20 minutes, flipping halfway through. Remove the patties and place them on a serving platter. Repeat with the remaining patties. 4. While the patties cook, make the tzatziki: Place all the ingredients in a small bowl and stir well. Cover and store in the fridge until ready to serve. Garnish with ground black pepper before serving. 5. Serve the patties with a dollop of tzatziki, a sprinkle of crumbled feta cheese, diced red onions, sliced black olives, and sliced cucumbers. 6. Store leftovers in an airtight container in the refrigerator for up to 5 days or in the freezer for up to a month. Reheat the patties in a preheated 200ºC air fryer for a few minutes, until warmed through.

Not-So-English Muffins

Prep time: 5 minutes | Cook time: 10 minutes | Serves 4

2 strips turkey bacon, cut in half crosswise
2 whole-grain English muffins, split
235 ml fresh baby spinach, long stems removed

¼ ripe pear, peeled and thinly sliced
4 slices low-moisture Mozzarella or other melting cheese

1. Place bacon strips in air fryer basket and air fry at 200ºC for 2 minutes. Check and separate strips if necessary so they cook evenly. Cook for 3 to 4 more minutes, until crispy. Remove and drain on paper towels. 2. Place split muffin halves in air fryer basket and cook for 2 minutes, just until lightly browned. 3. Open air fryer and top each muffin with a quarter of the baby spinach, several pear slices, a strip of bacon, and a slice of cheese. 4. Air fry at 182ºC for 1 to 2 minutes, until cheese completely melts.

Breakfast Sausage and Cauliflower

Prep time: 5 minutes | Cook time: 45 minutes | Serves 4

450 g sausage meat, cooked and crumbled
475 ml double/whipping cream
1 head cauliflower, chopped
235 ml grated Cheddar cheese,

plus more for topping
8 eggs, beaten
Salt and ground black pepper, to taste

1. Preheat the air fryer to 176°C. 2. In a large bowl, mix the sausage, cream, chopped cauliflower, cheese and eggs. Sprinkle with salt and ground black pepper. 3. Pour the mixture into a greased casserole dish. Bake in the preheated air fryer for 45 minutes or until firm. 4. Top with more Cheddar cheese and serve.

Classic British Breakfast

Prep time: 5 minutes | Cook time: 25 minutes | Serves 2

235 ml potatoes, sliced and diced
475 ml baked beans
2 eggs

1 tablespoon olive oil
1 sausage
Salt, to taste

1. Preheat the air fryer to 200°C and allow to warm. 2. Break the eggs onto a baking dish and sprinkle with salt. 3. Lay the beans on the dish, next to the eggs. 4. In a bowl, coat the potatoes with the olive oil. Sprinkle with salt. 5. Transfer the bowl of potato slices to the air fryer and bake for 10 minutes. 6. Swap out the bowl of potatoes for the dish containing the eggs and beans. Bake for another 10 minutes. Cover the potatoes with parchment paper. 7. Slice up the sausage and throw the slices on top of the beans and eggs. Bake for another 5 minutes. 8. Serve with the potatoes.

Tomato and Cheddar Rolls

Prep time: 30 minutes | Cook time: 25 minutes | Makes 12 rolls

4 plum tomatoes
½ clove garlic, minced
1 tablespoon olive oil
¼ teaspoon dried thyme
Salt and freshly ground black pepper, to taste
1 L plain flour
1 teaspoon active dry yeast

2 teaspoons sugar
2 teaspoons salt
1 tablespoon olive oil
235 ml grated Cheddar cheese, plus more for sprinkling at the end
350 ml water

1. Cut the tomatoes in half, remove the seeds with your fingers and transfer to a bowl. Add the garlic, olive oil, dried thyme, salt and freshly ground black pepper and toss well. 2. Preheat the air fryer to 200°C. 3. Place the tomatoes, cut side up in the air fryer basket and air fry for 10 minutes. The tomatoes should just start to brown. Shake the basket to redistribute the tomatoes, and air fry for another 5 to 10 minutes at 166°C until the tomatoes are no longer juicy. Let the tomatoes cool and then rough chop them. 4. Combine the flour, yeast, sugar and salt in the bowl of a stand mixer. Add the olive oil, chopped roasted tomatoes and Cheddar cheese to the flour mixture and start to mix using the dough hook attachment. As you're mixing, add 300 ml of the water, mixing until the dough comes together. Continue to knead the dough with the dough hook for another 10 minutes, adding enough water to the dough to get it to the right consistency. 5. Transfer the dough to an oiled bowl, cover with a clean kitchen towel and let it rest and rise until it has doubled in volume, about 1 to 2 hours. Then, divide the dough into 12 equal portions. Roll each portion of dough into a ball. Lightly coat each dough ball with oil and let the dough balls rest and rise a second time, covered lightly with plastic wrap for 45 minutes. (Alternately, you can place the rolls in the refrigerator overnight and take them out 2 hours before you bake them.) 6. Preheat the air fryer to 182°C. 7. Spray the dough balls and the air fryer basket with a little olive oil. Place three rolls at a time in the basket and bake for 10 minutes. Add a little grated Cheddar cheese on top of the rolls for the last 2 minutes of air frying for an attractive finish.

Apple Rolls

Prep time: 20 minutes | Cook time: 20 to 24 minutes | Makes 12 rolls

Apple Rolls:
475 ml plain flour, plus more for dusting
2 tablespoons granulated sugar
1 teaspoon salt
3 tablespoons butter, at room temperature
180 ml milk, whole or semi-skimmed
120 ml packed light brown

sugar
1 teaspoon ground cinnamon
1 large Granny Smith apple, peeled and diced
1 to 2 tablespoons oil
Icing:
120 ml icing sugar
½ teaspoon vanilla extract
2 to 3 tablespoons milk, whole or semi-skimmed

Make the Apple Rolls 1. In a large bowl, whisk the flour, granulated sugar, and salt until blended. Stir in the butter and milk briefly until a sticky dough forms. 2. In a small bowl, stir together the brown sugar, cinnamon, and apple. 3. Place a piece of parchment paper on a work surface and dust it with flour. Roll the dough on the prepared surface to ¼ inch thickness. 4. Spread the apple mixture over the dough. Roll up the dough jelly roll-style, pinching the ends to seal. Cut the dough into 12 rolls. 5. Preheat the air fryer to 160°C. 6. Line the air fryer basket with parchment paper and spritz it with oil. Place 6 rolls on the prepared parchment. 7. Bake for 5 minutes. Flip the rolls and bake for 5 to 7 minutes more until lightly browned. Repeat with the remaining rolls. Make the Icing 8. In a medium bowl, whisk the icing sugar, vanilla, and milk until blended. 9. Drizzle over the warm rolls.

Southwestern Ham Egg Cups

Prep time: 5 minutes | Cook time: 12 minutes | Serves 2

4 (30 g) slices wafer-thin ham
4 large eggs
2 tablespoons full-fat sour cream
60 ml diced green pepper
2 tablespoons diced red pepper
2 tablespoons diced brown onion
120 ml shredded medium Cheddar cheese

1. Place one slice of ham on the bottom of four baking cups. 2. In a large bowl, whisk eggs with sour cream. Stir in green pepper, red pepper, and onion. 3. Pour the egg mixture into ham-lined baking cups. Top with Cheddar. Place cups into the air fryer basket. 4. Adjust the temperature to 160ºC and bake for 12 minutes or until the tops are browned. 5. Serve warm.

Hearty Cheddar Biscuits

Prep time: 10 minutes | Cook time: 22 minutes | Makes 8 biscuits

550 ml self-raising flour
2 tablespoons sugar
120 ml butter, frozen for 15 minutes
120 ml grated Cheddar cheese,
plus more to melt on top
315 ml buttermilk
235 ml plain flour, for shaping
1 tablespoon butter, melted

1. Line a buttered 7-inch metal cake pan with parchment paper or a silicone liner. 2. Combine the flour and sugar in a large mixing bowl. Grate the butter into the flour. Add the grated cheese and stir to coat the cheese and butter with flour. Then add the buttermilk and stir just until you can no longer see streaks of flour. The dough should be quite wet. 3. Spread the plain (not self-raising) flour out on a small cookie sheet. With a spoon, scoop 8 evenly sized balls of dough into the flour, making sure they don't touch each other. With floured hands, coat each dough ball with flour and toss them gently from hand to hand to shake off any excess flour. Put each floured dough ball into the prepared pan, right up next to the other. This will help the biscuits rise, rather than spreading out. 4. Preheat the air fryer to 192ºC. 5. Transfer the cake pan to the basket of the air fryer. Let the ends of the aluminum foil sling hang across the cake pan before returning the basket to the air fryer. 6. Air fry for 20 minutes. Check the biscuits twice to make sure they are not getting too brown on top. If they are, re-arrange the aluminum foil strips to cover any brown parts. After 20 minutes, check the biscuits by inserting a toothpick into the center of the biscuits. It should come out clean. If it needs a little more time, continue to air fry for two extra minutes. Brush the tops of the biscuits with some melted butter and sprinkle a little more grated cheese on top if desired. Pop the basket back into the air fryer for another 2 minutes. 7. Remove the cake pan from the air fryer. Let the biscuits cool for just a minute or two and then turn them out onto a plate and pull apart. Serve immediately.

Sirloin Steaks with Eggs

Prep time: 8 minutes | Cook time: 14 minutes per batch | Serves 4

Cooking oil spray
4 (110 g) sirloin steaks
1 teaspoon granulated garlic, divided
1 teaspoon salt, divided
1 teaspoon freshly ground black pepper, divided
4 eggs
½ teaspoon paprika

1. Insert the crisper plate into the basket and the basket into the unit. Preheat the unit by selecting AIR FRY, setting the temperature to 182ºC, and setting the time to 3 minutes. Select START/STOP to begin. 2. Once the unit is preheated, spray the crisper plate with cooking oil. Place 2 steaks into the basket; do not oil or season them at this time. 3. Select AIR FRY, set the temperature to 182ºC, and set the time to 9 minutes. Select START/STOP to begin. 4. After 5 minutes, open the unit and flip the steaks. Sprinkle each with ¼ teaspoon of granulated garlic, ¼ teaspoon of salt, and ¼ teaspoon of pepper. Resume cooking until the steaks register at least 64ºC on a food thermometer. 5. When the cooking is complete, transfer the steaks to a plate and tent with aluminum foil to keep warm. Repeat steps 2, 3, and 4 with the remaining steaks. 6. Spray 4 ramekins with olive oil. Crack 1 egg into each ramekin. Sprinkle the eggs with the paprika and remaining ½ teaspoon each of salt and pepper. Working in batches, place 2 ramekins into the basket. 7. Select BAKE, set the temperature to 166ºC, and set the time to 5 minutes. Select START/STOP to begin. 8. When the cooking is complete and the eggs are cooked to 72ºC, remove the ramekins and repeat step 7 with the remaining 2 ramekins. 9. Serve the eggs with the steaks.

Three-Berry Dutch Pancake

Prep time: 10 minutes | Cook time: 12 to 16 minutes | Serves 4

2 egg whites
1 egg
120 ml wholemeal plain flour plus 1 tablespoon cornflour
120 ml semi-skimmed milk
1 teaspoon pure vanilla extract
1 tablespoon unsalted butter, melted
235 ml sliced fresh strawberries
120 ml fresh blueberries
120 ml fresh raspberries

1. In a medium bowl, use an eggbeater or hand mixer to quickly mix the egg whites, egg, flour, milk, and vanilla until well combined. 2. Use a pastry brush to grease the bottom of a baking pan with the melted butter. Immediately pour in the batter and put the basket back in the fryer. Bake at 166ºC for 12 to 16 minutes, or until the pancake is puffed and golden brown. 3. Remove the pan from the air fryer; the pancake will fall. Top with the strawberries, blueberries, and raspberries. Serve immediately.

Breakfast Calzone

Prep time: 15 minutes | Cook time: 15 minutes | Serves 4

350 ml shredded Mozzarella cheese
120 ml blanched finely ground almond flour
30 g full-fat cream cheese
1 large whole egg

4 large eggs, scrambled
230 g cooked sausage meat, removed from casings and crumbled
8 tablespoons shredded mild Cheddar cheese

1. In a large microwave-safe bowl, add Mozzarella, almond flour, and cream cheese. Microwave for 1 minute. Stir until the mixture is smooth and forms a ball. Add the egg and stir until dough forms. 2. Place dough between two sheets of parchment and roll out to ¼-inch thickness. Cut the dough into four rectangles. 3. Mix scrambled eggs and cooked sausage together in a large bowl. Divide the mixture evenly among each piece of dough, placing it on the lower half of the rectangle. Sprinkle each with 2 tablespoons Cheddar. 4. Fold over the rectangle to cover the egg and meat mixture. Pinch, roll, or use a wet fork to close the edges completely. 5. Cut a piece of parchment to fit your air fryer basket and place the calzones onto the parchment. Place parchment into the air fryer basket. 6. Adjust the temperature to 192°C and air fry for 15 minutes. 7. Flip the calzones halfway through the cooking time. When done, calzones should be golden in color. Serve immediately.

Parmesan Ranch Risotto

Prep time: 10 minutes | Cook time: 30 minutes | Serves 2

1 tablespoon olive oil
1 clove garlic, minced
1 tablespoon unsalted butter
1 onion, diced

180 ml Arborio rice
475 ml chicken stock, boiling
120 ml Parmesan cheese, grated

1. Preheat the air fryer to 200°C. 2. Grease a round baking tin with olive oil and stir in the garlic, butter, and onion. 3. Transfer the tin to the air fryer and bake for 4 minutes. Add the rice and bake for 4 more minutes. 4. Turn the air fryer to 160°C and pour in the chicken stock. Cover and bake for 22 minutes. 5. Scatter with cheese and serve.

Bacon Eggs on the Go

Prep time: 5 minutes | Cook time: 15 minutes | Serves 1

2 eggs
110 g bacon, cooked

Salt and ground black pepper, to taste

1. Preheat the air fryer to 204°C. Put liners in a regular cupcake tin. 2. Crack an egg into each of the cups and add the bacon. Season with some pepper and salt. 3. Bake in the preheated air fryer for 15 minutes, or until the eggs are set. Serve warm.

Tomato and Mozzarella Bruschetta

Prep time: 5 minutes | Cook time: 4 minutes | Serves 1

6 small loaf slices
120 ml tomatoes, finely chopped
85 g Mozzarella cheese, grated

1 tablespoon fresh basil, chopped
1 tablespoon olive oil

1. Preheat the air fryer to 176°C. 2. Put the loaf slices inside the air fryer and air fry for about 3 minutes. 3. Add the tomato, Mozzarella, basil, and olive oil on top. 4. Air fry for an additional minute before serving.

Fried Chicken Wings with Waffles

Prep time: 10 minutes | Cook time: 30 minutes | Serves 4

8 whole chicken wings
1 teaspoon garlic powder
Chicken seasoning, for preparing the chicken
Freshly ground black pepper, to taste

120 ml plain flour
Cooking oil spray
8 frozen waffles
Pure maple syrup, for serving (optional)

1. In a medium bowl, combine the chicken and garlic powder and season with chicken seasoning and pepper. Toss to coat. 2. Transfer the chicken to a resealable plastic bag and add the flour. Seal the bag and shake it to coat the chicken thoroughly. 3. Insert the crisper plate into the basket and the basket into the unit. Preheat the unit by selecting AIR FRY, setting the temperature to 204°C, and setting the time to 3 minutes. Select START/STOP to begin. 4. Once the unit is preheated, spray the crisper plate with cooking oil. Using tongs, transfer the chicken from the bag to the basket. It is okay to stack the chicken wings on top of each other. Spray them with cooking oil. 5. Select AIR FRY, set the temperature to 204°C, and set the time to 20 minutes. Select START/STOP to begin. 6. After 5 minutes, remove the basket and shake the wings. Reinsert the basket to resume cooking. Remove and shake the basket every 5 minutes until the chicken is fully cooked. 7. When the cooking is complete, remove the cooked chicken from the basket; cover to keep warm. 8. Rinse the basket and crisper plate with warm water. Insert them back into the unit. 9. Select AIR FRY, set the temperature to 182°C, and set the time to 3 minutes. Select START/STOP to begin. 10. Once the unit is preheated, spray the crisper plate with cooking spray. Working in batches, place the frozen waffles into the basket. Do not stack them. Spray the waffles with cooking oil. 11. Select AIR FRY, set the temperature to 182°C, and set the time to 6 minutes. Select START/STOP to begin. 12. When the cooking is complete, repeat steps 10 and 11 with the remaining waffles. 13. Serve the waffles with the chicken and a touch of maple syrup, if desired.

Spinach and Mushroom Mini Quiche

Prep time: 10 minutes | Cook time: 15 minutes | Serves 4

1 teaspoon olive oil, plus more for spraying
235 ml coarsely chopped mushrooms
235 ml fresh baby spinach, shredded
4 eggs, beaten

120 ml shredded Cheddar cheese
120 ml shredded Mozzarella cheese
¼ teaspoon salt
¼ teaspoon black pepper

1. Spray 4 silicone baking cups with olive oil and set aside. 2. In a medium sauté pan over medium heat, warm 1 teaspoon of olive oil. Add the mushrooms and sauté until soft, 3 to 4 minutes. 3. Add the spinach and cook until wilted, 1 to 2 minutes. Set aside. 4. In a medium bowl, whisk together the eggs, Cheddar cheese, Mozzarella cheese, salt, and pepper. 5. Gently fold the mushrooms and spinach into the egg mixture. 6. Pour ¼ of the mixture into each silicone baking cup. 7. Place the baking cups into the air fryer basket and air fry at 176°C for 5 minutes. Stir the mixture in each ramekin slightly and air fry until the egg has set, an additional 3 to 5 minutes.

Bacon-and-Eggs Avocado

Prep time: 5 minutes | Cook time: 17 minutes | Serves 1

1 large egg
1 avocado, halved, peeled, and pitted
2 slices bacon

Fresh parsley, for serving (optional)
Sea salt flakes, for garnish (optional)

1. Spray the air fryer basket with avocado oil. Preheat the air fryer to 160°C. Fill a small bowl with cool water. 2. Soft-boil the egg: Place the egg in the air fryer basket. Air fry for 6 minutes for a soft yolk or 7 minutes for a cooked yolk. Transfer the egg to the bowl of cool water and let sit for 2 minutes. Peel and set aside. 3. Use a spoon to carve out extra space in the center of the avocado halves until the cavities are big enough to fit the soft-boiled egg. Place the soft-boiled egg in the center of one half of the avocado and replace the other half of the avocado on top, so the avocado appears whole on the outside. 4. Starting at one end of the avocado, wrap the bacon around the avocado to completely cover it. Use toothpicks to hold the bacon in place. 5. Place the bacon-wrapped avocado in the air fryer basket and air fry for 5 minutes. Flip the avocado over and air fry for another 5 minutes, or until the bacon is cooked to your liking. Serve on a bed of fresh parsley, if desired, and sprinkle with salt flakes, if desired. 6. Best served fresh. Store extras in an airtight container in the fridge for up to 4 days. Reheat in a preheated 160°C air fryer for 4 minutes, or until heated through.

Italian Egg Cups

Prep time: 5 minutes | Cook time: 10 minutes | Serves 4

Olive oil
235 ml marinara sauce
4 eggs
4 tablespoons shredded Mozzarella cheese

4 teaspoons grated Parmesan cheese
Salt and freshly ground black pepper, to taste
Chopped fresh basil, for garnish

1. Lightly spray 4 individual ramekins with olive oil. 2. Pour 60 ml marinara sauce into each ramekin. 3. Crack one egg into each ramekin on top of the marinara sauce. 4. Sprinkle 1 tablespoon of Mozzarella and 1 tablespoon of Parmesan on top of each egg. Season with salt and pepper. 5. Cover each ramekin with aluminum foil. Place two of the ramekins in the air fryer basket. 6. Air fry at 176°C for 5 minutes and remove the aluminum foil. Air fry until the top is lightly browned and the egg white is cooked, another 2 to 4 minutes. If you prefer the yolk to be firmer, cook for 3 to 5 more minutes. 7. Repeat with the remaining two ramekins. Garnish with basil and serve.

Western Frittata

Prep time: 10 minutes | Cook time: 19 minutes | Serves 1 to 2

½ red or green pepper, cut into ½-inch chunks
1 teaspoon olive oil
3 eggs, beaten
60 ml grated Cheddar cheese
60 ml diced cooked ham

Salt and freshly ground black pepper, to taste
1 teaspoon butter
1 teaspoon chopped fresh parsley

1. Preheat the air fryer to 204°C. 2. Toss the peppers with the olive oil and air fry for 6 minutes, shaking the basket once or twice during the cooking process to redistribute the ingredients. 3. While the vegetables are cooking, beat the eggs well in a bowl, stir in the Cheddar cheese and ham, and season with salt and freshly ground black pepper. Add the air-fried peppers to this bowl when they have finished cooking. 4. Place a cake pan into the air fryer basket with the butter using an aluminum sling to lower the pan into the basket. Air fry for 1 minute at 192°C to melt the butter. Remove the cake pan and rotate the pan to distribute the butter and grease the pan. Pour the egg mixture into the cake pan and return the pan to the air fryer, using the aluminum sling. 5. Air fry at 192°C for 12 minutes, or until the frittata has puffed up and is lightly browned. Let the frittata sit in the air fryer for 5 minutes to cool to an edible temperature and set up. Remove the cake pan from the air fryer, sprinkle with parsley and serve immediately.

Egg and Bacon Muffins

Prep time: 5 minutes | Cook time: 15 minutes | Serves 1

2 eggs
Salt and ground black pepper,
to taste
1 tablespoon green pesto

85 g shredded Cheddar cheese
140 g cooked bacon
1 spring onion, chopped

1. Preheat the air fryer to 176ºC. Line a cupcake tin with parchment paper. 2. Beat the eggs with pepper, salt, and pesto in a bowl. Mix in the cheese. 3. Pour the eggs into the cupcake tin and top with the bacon and spring onion. 4. Bake in the preheated air fryer for 15 minutes, or until the egg is set. 5. Serve immediately.

Spinach and Bacon Roll-ups

Prep time: 5 minutes | Cook time: 8 to 9 minutes | Serves 4

4 flour tortillas (6- or 7-inch
size)
4 slices Swiss cheese
235 ml baby spinach leaves

4 slices turkey bacon
Special Equipment:
4 toothpicks, soak in water for
at least 30 minutes

1. Preheat the air fryer to 200ºC. 2. On a clean work surface, top each tortilla with one slice of cheese and 60 ml spinach, then tightly roll them up. 3. Wrap each tortilla with a strip of turkey bacon and secure with a toothpick. 4. Arrange the roll-ups in the air fryer basket, leaving space between each roll-up. 5. Air fry for 4 minutes. Flip the roll-ups with tongs and rearrange them for more even cooking. Air fry for another 4 to 5 minutes until the bacon is crisp. 6. Rest for 5 minutes and remove the toothpicks before serving.

Lemon-Blueberry Muffins

Prep time: 5 minutes | Cook time: 20 to 25 minutes | Makes 6

muffins
300 ml almond flour
3 tablespoons granulated
sweetener
1 teaspoon baking powder
2 large eggs

3 tablespoons melted butter
1 tablespoon almond milk
1 tablespoon fresh lemon juice
120 ml fresh blueberries

1. Preheat the air fryer to 176ºC. Lightly coat 6 silicone muffin cups with vegetable oil. Set aside. 2. In a large mixing bowl, combine the almond flour, sweetener, and baking soda. Set aside. 3. In a separate small bowl, whisk together the eggs, butter, milk, and lemon juice. Add the egg mixture to the flour mixture and stir until just combined. Fold in the blueberries and let the batter sit for 5 minutes. 4. Spoon the muffin batter into the muffin cups, about two-

thirds full. Air fry for 20 to 25 minutes, or until a toothpick inserted into the center of a muffin comes out clean. 5. Remove the basket from the air fryer and let the muffins cool for about 5 minutes before transferring them to a wire rack to cool completely.

Banana-Nut Muffins

Prep time: 5 minutes | Cook time: 15 minutes | Makes 10 muffins

Oil, for spraying
2 very ripe bananas
120 ml packed light brown
sugar
80 ml rapeseed oil or vegetable
oil

1 large egg
1 teaspoon vanilla extract
180 ml plain flour
1 teaspoon baking powder
1 teaspoon ground cinnamon
120 ml chopped walnuts

1. Preheat the air fryer to 160ºC. Spray 10 silicone muffin cups lightly with oil. 2. In a medium bowl, mash the bananas. Add the brown sugar, rapeseed oil, egg, and vanilla and stir to combine. 3. Fold in the flour, baking powder, and cinnamon until just combined. 4. Add the walnuts and fold a few times to distribute throughout the batter. 5. Divide the batter equally among the prepared muffin cups and place them in the basket. You may need to work in batches, depending on the size of your air fryer. 6. Cook for 15 minutes, or until golden brown and a toothpick inserted into the center of a muffin comes out clean. The air fryer tends to brown muffins more than the oven, so don't be alarmed if they are darker than you're used to. They will still taste great. 7. Let cool on a wire rack before serving.

Ham and Cheese Crescents

Prep time: 5 minutes | Cook time: 7 minutes | Makes 8 rolls

Oil, for spraying
1 (230 g) can ready-to-bake
croissants
4 slices wafer-thin ham

8 cheese slices
2 tablespoons unsalted butter,
melted

1. Line the air fryer basket with parchment and spray lightly with oil. 2. Separate the dough into 8 pieces. 3. Tear the ham slices in half and place 1 piece on each piece of dough. Top each with 1 slice of cheese. 4. Roll up each piece of dough, starting on the wider side. 5. Place the rolls in the prepared basket. Brush with the melted butter. 6. Air fry at 160ºC for 6 to 7 minutes, or until puffed and golden brown and the cheese is melted.

Drop Biscuits

Prep time: 10 minutes | Cook time: 9 to 10 minutes | Serves 5

1 L plain flour
1 tablespoon baking powder
1 tablespoon sugar (optional)
1 teaspoon salt
6 tablespoons butter, plus more

for brushing on the biscuits
(optional)
180 ml buttermilk
1 to 2 tablespoons oil

1. In a large bowl, whisk the flour, baking powder, sugar (if using), and salt until blended. 2. Add the butter. Using a pastry cutter or 2 forks, work the dough until pea-size balls of the butter-flour mixture appear. Stir in the buttermilk until the mixture is sticky. 3. Preheat the air fryer to 166°C. Line the air fryer basket with parchment paper and spritz it with oil. 4. Drop the dough by the tablespoonful onto the prepared basket, leaving 1 inch between each, to form 10 biscuits. 5. Bake for 5 minutes. Flip the biscuits and cook for 4 minutes more for a light brown top, or 5 minutes more for a darker biscuit. Brush the tops with melted butter, if desired.

Baked Potato Breakfast Boats

Prep time: 10 minutes | Cook time: 20 minutes | Serves 4

2 large white potatoes, scrubbed
Olive oil
Salt and freshly ground black
pepper, to taste
4 eggs

2 tablespoons chopped, cooked
bacon
235 ml shredded Cheddar
cheese

1. Poke holes in the potatoes with a fork and microwave on full power for 5 minutes. 2. Turn potatoes over and cook an additional 3 to 5 minutes, or until the potatoes are fork-tender. 3. Cut the potatoes in half lengthwise and use a spoon to scoop out the inside of the potato. Be careful to leave a layer of potato so that it makes a sturdy "boat." 4. Preheat the air fryer to 176°C. 5. Lightly spray the air fryer basket with olive oil. Spray the skin side of the potatoes with oil and sprinkle with salt and pepper to taste. 6. Place the potato skins in the air fryer basket, skin-side down. Crack one egg into each potato skin. 7. Sprinkle ½ tablespoon of bacon pieces and 60 ml shredded cheese on top of each egg. Sprinkle with salt and pepper to taste. 8. Air fry until the yolk is slightly runny, 5 to 6 minutes, or until the yolk is fully cooked, 7 to 10 minutes.

Scotch Eggs

Prep time: 10 minutes | Cook time: 20 to 25 minutes | Serves 4

2 tablespoons flour, plus extra
for coating
450 g sausage meat
4 hard-boiled eggs, peeled
1 raw egg

1 tablespoon water
Oil for misting or cooking spray
Crumb Coating:
180 ml panko bread crumbs
180 ml flour

1. Combine flour with sausage meat and mix thoroughly. 2. Divide into 4 equal portions and mold each around a hard-boiled egg so the sausage completely covers the egg. 3. In a small bowl, beat together the raw egg and water. 4. Dip sausage-covered eggs in the remaining flour, then the egg mixture, then roll in the crumb coating. 5. Air fry at 182°C for 10 minutes. Spray eggs, turn, and spray other side. 6. Continue cooking for another 10 to 15 minutes or until sausage is well done.

Mozzarella Bacon Calzones

Prep time: 15 minutes | Cook time: 12 minutes | Serves 4

2 large eggs
235 ml blanched finely ground
almond flour
475 ml shredded Mozzarella
cheese

60 g cream cheese, softened
and broken into small pieces
4 slices cooked bacon,
crumbled

1. Beat eggs in a small bowl. Pour into a medium nonstick skillet over medium heat and scramble. Set aside. 2. In a large microwave-safe bowl, mix flour and Mozzarella. Add cream cheese to the bowl. 3. Place bowl in microwave and cook 45 seconds on high to melt cheese, then stir with a fork until a soft dough ball forms. 4. Cut a piece of parchment to fit air fryer basket. Separate dough into two sections and press each out into an 8-inch round. 5. On half of each dough round, place half of the scrambled eggs and crumbled bacon. Fold the other side of the dough over and press to seal the edges. 6. Place calzones on ungreased parchment and into air fryer basket. Adjust the temperature to 176°C and set the timer for 12 minutes, turning calzones halfway through cooking. Crust will be golden and firm when done. 7. Let calzones cool on a cooking rack 5 minutes before serving.

Chapter 2 Snacks and Appetizers

Garlic-Parmesan Croutons

Prep time: 3 minutes | Cook time: 12 minutes | Serves 4

Oil, for spraying
1 L cubed French bread
1 tablespoon grated Parmesan
cheese

3 tablespoons olive oil
1 tablespoon granulated garlic
½ teaspoon unsalted salt

1. Line the air fryer basket with parchment and spray lightly with oil. 2. In a large bowl, mix together the bread, Parmesan cheese, olive oil, garlic, and salt, tossing with your hands to evenly distribute the seasonings. Transfer the coated bread cubes to the prepared basket. 3. Air fry at 176ºC for 10 to 12 minutes, stirring once after 5 minutes, or until crisp and golden brown.

Root Veggie Chips with Herb Salt

Prep time: 10 minutes | Cook time: 8 minutes | Serves 2

1 parsnip, washed
1 small beetroot, washed
1 small turnip, washed
½ small sweet potato, washed
1 teaspoon olive oil

Cooking spray
Herb Salt:
¼ teaspoon rock salt
2 teaspoons finely chopped
fresh parsley

1. Preheat the air fryer to 182ºC. 2. Peel and thinly slice the parsnip, beetroot, turnip, and sweet potato, then place the vegetables in a large bowl, add the olive oil, and toss. 3. Spray the air fryer basket with cooking spray, then place the vegetables in the basket and air fry for 8 minutes, gently shaking the basket halfway through. 4. While the chips cook, make the herb salt in a small bowl by combining the rock salt and parsley. 5. Remove the chips and place on a serving plate, then sprinkle the herb salt on top and allow to cool for 2 to 3 minutes before serving.

Spiralized Potato Nest with Tomato Ketchup

Prep time: 10 minutes | Cook time: 15 minutes | Serves 2

1 large russet or Maris Piper
potato (about 340 g)
2 tablespoons vegetable oil
1 tablespoon hot smoked
paprika
½ teaspoon garlic powder

Rock salt and freshly ground
black pepper, to taste
120 ml canned crushed
tomatoes
2 tablespoons apple cider
vinegar

1 tablespoon dark brown sugar
1 tablespoon Worcestershire

sauce
1 teaspoon mild hot sauce

1. Using a spiralizer, spiralize the potato, then place in a large colander. (If you don't have a spiralizer, cut the potato into thin ⅛-inch-thick matchsticks.) Rinse the potatoes under cold running water until the water runs clear. Spread the potatoes out on a double-thick layer of paper towels and pat completely dry. 2. In a large bowl, combine the potatoes, oil, paprika, and garlic powder. Season with salt and pepper and toss to combine. Transfer the potatoes to the air fryer and air fry at 204ºC until the potatoes are browned and crisp, 15 minutes, shaking the basket halfway through. 3. Meanwhile, in a small blender, purée the tomatoes, vinegar, brown sugar, Worcestershire, and hot sauce until smooth. Pour into a small saucepan or skillet and simmer over medium heat until reduced by half, 3 to 5 minutes. Pour the homemade ketchup into a bowl and let cool. 4. Remove the spiralized potato nest from the air fryer and serve hot with the ketchup.

Cheese-Stuffed Blooming Onion

Prep time: 10 minutes | Cook time: 15 minutes | Serves 2

1 large brown onion (397 g)
1 tablespoon olive oil
Rock salt and freshly ground
black pepper, to taste
60 ml plus 2 tablespoons panko
breadcrumbs
60 ml grated Parmesan cheese

3 tablespoons mayonnaise
1 tablespoon fresh lemon juice
1 tablespoon chopped fresh flat-
leaf parsley
2 teaspoons whole-grain Dijon
mustard
1 garlic clove, minced

1. Place the onion on a cutting board and trim the top off and peel off the outer skin. Turn the onion upside down and use a paring knife, cut vertical slits halfway through the onion at ½-inch intervals around the onion, keeping the root intact. When you turn the onion right side up, it should open up like the petals of a flower. Drizzle the cut sides of the onion with the olive oil and season with salt and pepper. Place petal-side up in the air fryer and air fry at 176ºC for 10 minutes. 2. Meanwhile, in a bowl, stir together the panko, Parmesan, mayonnaise, lemon juice, parsley, mustard, and garlic until incorporated into a smooth paste. 3. Remove the onion from the fryer and stuff the paste all over and in between the onion "petals." Return the onion to the air fryer and air fry at 192ºC until the onion is tender in the centre and the bread crumb mixture is golden brown, about 5 minutes. Remove the onion from the air fryer, transfer to a plate, and serve hot.

Pepperoni Pizza Dip

Prep time: 10 minutes | Cook time: 10 minutes | Serves 6

170 g soft white cheese
177 ml shredded Italian cheese blend
60 ml sour cream
1½ teaspoons dried Italian seasoning
¼ teaspoon garlic salt
¼ teaspoon onion powder
177 ml pizza sauce

120 ml sliced miniature pepperoni
60 ml sliced black olives
1 tablespoon thinly sliced green onion
Cut-up raw vegetables, toasted baguette slices, pitta chips, or tortilla chips, for serving

1. In a small bowl, combine the soft white cheese, 60 ml of the shredded cheese, the sour cream, Italian seasoning, garlic salt, and onion powder. Stir until smooth and the ingredients are well blended. 2. Spread the mixture in a baking pan. Top with the pizza sauce, spreading to the edges. Sprinkle with the remaining 120 ml shredded cheese. Arrange the pepperoni slices on top of the cheese. Top with the black olives and green onion. 3. Place the pan in the air fryer basket. Set the air fryer to 176ºC for 10 minutes, or until the pepperoni is beginning to brown on the edges and the cheese is bubbly and lightly browned. 4. Let stand for 5 minutes before serving with vegetables, toasted baguette slices, pitta chips, or tortilla chips.

Caramelized Onion Dip with White Cheese

Prep time: 5 minutes | Cook time: 30 minutes | Serves 8 to 10

1 tablespoon butter
1 medium onion, halved and thinly sliced
¼ teaspoon rock salt, plus additional for seasoning
113 g soft white cheese
120 ml sour cream

¼ teaspoon onion powder
1 tablespoon chopped fresh chives
Black pepper, to taste
Thick-cut potato crisps or vegetable crisps

1. Place the butter in a baking pan. Place the pan in the air fryer basket. Set the air fryer to 92ºC for 1 minute, or until the butter is melted. Add the onions and salt to the pan. 2. Set the air fryer to 92ºC for 15 minutes, or until onions are softened. Set the air fryer to 192ºC for 15 minutes, until onions are a deep golden brown, stirring two or three times during the cooking time. Let cool completely. 3. In a medium bowl, stir together the cooked onions, soft white cheese, sour cream, onion powder, and chives. Season with salt and pepper. Cover and refrigerate for 2 hours to allow the flavours to blend. 4. Serve the dip with potato crisps or vegetable crisps.

Old Bay Chicken Wings

Prep time: 10 minutes | Cook time: 12 to 15 minutes | Serves 4

2 tablespoons Old Bay or all-purpose seasoning
2 teaspoons baking powder

2 teaspoons salt
900 g chicken wings, patted dry
Cooking spray

1. Preheat the air fryer to 204ºC. Lightly spray the air fryer basket with cooking spray. 2. Combine the seasoning, baking powder, and salt in a large zip-top plastic bag. Add the chicken wings, seal, and shake until the wings are thoroughly coated in the seasoning mixture. 3. Lay the chicken wings in the air fryer basket in a single layer and lightly mist with cooking spray. You may need to work in batches to avoid overcrowding. 4. Air fry for 12 to 15 minutes, flipping the wings halfway through, or until the wings are lightly browned and the internal temperature reaches at least 74ºC on a meat thermometer. 5. Remove from the basket to a plate and repeat with the remaining chicken wings. 6. Serve hot.

Authentic Scotch Eggs

Prep time: 15 minutes | Cook time: 11 to 13 minutes | Serves 6

680 g bulk lean chicken or turkey sausage
3 raw eggs, divided
355 ml dried breadcrumbs,

divided
120 ml plain flour
6 hardboiled eggs, peeled
Cooking oil spray

1. In a large bowl, combine the chicken sausage, 1 raw egg, and 120 ml of breadcrumbs and mix well. Divide the mixture into 6 pieces and flatten each into a long oval. 2. In a shallow bowl, beat the remaining 2 raw eggs. 3. Place the flour in a small bowl. 4. Place the remaining 240 ml of breadcrumbs in a second small bowl. 5. Roll each hardboiled egg in the flour and wrap one of the chicken sausage pieces around each egg to encircle it completely. 6. One at a time, roll the encased eggs in the flour, dip in the beaten eggs, and finally dip in the breadcrumbs to coat. 7. Insert the crisper plate into the basket and the basket into the unit. Preheat the unit by selecting AIR FRY, setting the temperature to 192ºC, and setting the time to 3 minutes. Select START/STOP to begin. 8. Once the unit is preheated, spray the crisper plate with cooking oil. Place the eggs in a single layer into the basket and spray them with oil. 9. Select AIR FRY, set the temperature to 192ºC, and set the time to 13 minutes. Select START/STOP to begin. 10. After about 6 minutes, use tongs to turn the eggs and spray them with more oil. Resume cooking for 5 to 7 minutes more, or until the chicken is thoroughly cooked and the Scotch eggs are browned. 11. When the cooking is complete, serve warm.

Black Bean Corn Dip

Prep time: 10 minutes | Cook time: 10 minutes | Serves 4

½ (425 g) can black beans, drained and rinsed
½ (425 g) can corn, drained and rinsed
60 ml chunky salsa
57 g low-fat soft white cheese
60 ml shredded low-fat Cheddar cheese
½ teaspoon ground cumin
½ teaspoon paprika
Salt and freshly ground black pepper, to taste

1. Preheat the air fryer to 164°C. 2. In a medium bowl, mix together the black beans, corn, salsa, soft white cheese, Cheddar cheese, cumin, and paprika. Season with salt and pepper and stir until well combined. 3. Spoon the mixture into a baking dish. 4. Place baking dish in the air fryer basket and bake until heated through, about 10 minutes. 5. Serve hot.

Crunchy Basil White Beans

Prep time: 2 minutes | Cook time: 19 minutes | Serves 2

1 (425 g) can cooked white beans
2 tablespoons olive oil
1 teaspoon fresh sage, chopped
¼ teaspoon garlic powder
¼ teaspoon salt, divided
1 teaspoon chopped fresh basil

1. Preheat the air fryer to 192°C. 2. In a medium bowl, mix together the beans, olive oil, sage, garlic, ⅛ teaspoon salt, and basil. 3. Pour the white beans into the air fryer and spread them out in a single layer. 4. Bake for 10 minutes. Stir and continue cooking for an additional 5 to 9 minutes, or until they reach your preferred level of crispiness. 5. Toss with the remaining ⅛ teaspoon salt before serving.

Five-Ingredient Falafel with Garlic-Yoghurt Sauce

Prep time: 5 minutes | Cook time: 15 minutes | Serves 4

Falafel:
1 (425 g) can chickpeas, drained and rinsed
120 ml fresh parsley
2 garlic cloves, minced
½ tablespoon ground cumin
1 tablespoon wholemeal flour
Salt
Garlic-Yoghurt Sauce:
240 ml non-fat plain Greek yoghurt
1 garlic clove, minced
1 tablespoon chopped fresh dill
2 tablespoons lemon juice

Make the Falafel: 1. Preheat the air fryer to 182°C. 2. Put the chickpeas into a food processor. Pulse until mostly chopped, then add the parsley, garlic, and cumin and pulse for another 1 to 2 minutes, or until the ingredients are combined and turning into a dough. 3. Add the flour. Pulse a few more times until combined.

The dough will have texture, but the chickpeas should be pulsed into small bits. 4. Using clean hands, roll the dough into 8 balls of equal size, then pat the balls down a bit so they are about ½-thick disks. 5. Spray the basket of the air fryer with olive oil cooking spray, then place the falafel patties in the basket in a single layer, making sure they don't touch each other. 6. Fry in the air fryer for 15 minutes. Make the garlic-yoghurt sauce 7. In a small bowl, combine the yoghurt, garlic, dill, and lemon juice. 8. Once the falafel is done cooking and nicely browned on all sides, remove them from the air fryer and season with salt. 9. Serve hot with a side of dipping sauce.

Feta and Quinoa Stuffed Mushrooms

Prep time: 5 minutes | Cook time: 8 minutes | Serves 6

2 tablespoons finely diced red pepper
1 garlic clove, minced
60 ml cooked quinoa
⅛ teaspoon salt
¼ teaspoon dried oregano
24 button mushrooms, stemmed
57 g crumbled feta
3 tablespoons wholemeal breadcrumbs
Olive oil cooking spray

1. Preheat the air fryer to 182°C. 2. In a small bowl, combine the pepper, garlic, quinoa, salt, and oregano. 3. Spoon the quinoa stuffing into the mushroom caps until just filled. 4. Add a small piece of feta to the top of each mushroom. 5. Sprinkle a pinch breadcrumbs over the feta on each mushroom. 6. Spray the basket of the air fryer with olive oil cooking spray, then gently place the mushrooms into the basket, making sure that they don't touch each other. (Depending on the size of the air fryer, you may have to cook them in two batches.) 7. Place the basket into the air fryer and bake for 8 minutes. 8. Remove from the air fryer and serve.

Easy Spiced Nuts

Prep time: 5 minutes | Cook time: 25 minutes | Makes 3 L

1 egg white, lightly beaten
60 ml sugar
1 teaspoon salt
½ teaspoon ground cinnamon
¼ teaspoon ground cloves
¼ teaspoon ground allspice
Pinch ground cayenne pepper
240 ml pecan halves
240 ml cashews
240 ml almonds

1. Combine the egg white with the sugar and spices in a bowl. 2. Preheat the air fryer to 148°C. 3. Spray or brush the air fryer basket with vegetable oil. Toss the nuts together in the spiced egg white and transfer the nuts to the air fryer basket. 4. Air fry for 25 minutes, stirring the nuts in the basket a few times during the cooking process. Taste the nuts (carefully because they will be very hot) to see if they are crunchy and nicely toasted. Air fry for a few more minutes if necessary. 5. Serve warm or cool to room temperature and store in an airtight container for up to two weeks.

Cinnamon-Apple Crisps

Prep time: 10 minutes | Cook time: 32 minutes | Serves 4

Oil, for spraying
2 Red Delicious or Honeycrisp apples

¼ teaspoon ground cinnamon, divided

1. Line the air fryer basket with parchment and spray lightly with oil. 2. Trim the uneven ends off the apples. Using a mandoline slicer on the thinnest setting or a sharp knife, cut the apples into very thin slices. Discard the cores. 3. Place half of the apple slices in a single layer in the prepared basket and sprinkle with half of the cinnamon. 4. Place a metal air fryer trivet on top of the apples to keep them from flying around while they are cooking. 5. Air fry at 148°C for 16 minutes, flipping every 5 minutes to ensure even cooking. Repeat with the remaining apple slices and cinnamon. 6. Let cool to room temperature before serving. The crisps will firm up as they cool.

Red Pepper Tapenade

Prep time: 5 minutes | Cook time: 5 minutes | Serves 4

1 large red pepper
2 tablespoons plus 1 teaspoon olive oil, divided
120 ml Kalamata olives, pitted

and roughly chopped
1 garlic clove, minced
½ teaspoon dried oregano
1 tablespoon lemon juice

1. Preheat the air fryer to 192°C. 2. Brush the outside of a whole red pepper with 1 teaspoon olive oil and place it inside the air fryer basket. Roast for 5 minutes. 3. Meanwhile, in a medium bowl combine the remaining 2 tablespoons of olive oil with the olives, garlic, oregano, and lemon juice. 4. Remove the red pepper from the air fryer, then gently slice off the stem and remove the seeds. Roughly chop the roasted pepper into small pieces. 5. Add the red pepper to the olive mixture and stir all together until combined. 6. Serve with pitta chips, crackers, or crusty bread.

Pork and Cabbage Egg Rolls

Prep time: 15 minutes | Cook time: 12 minutes | Makes 12 egg rolls

Cooking oil spray
2 garlic cloves, minced
340 g minced pork
1 teaspoon sesame oil
60 ml soy sauce
2 teaspoons grated peeled fresh

ginger
475 ml shredded green cabbage
4 spring onions, green parts (white parts optional), chopped
24 egg roll wrappers

1. Spray a skillet with the cooking oil and place it over medium-high heat. Add the garlic and cook for 1 minute until fragrant. 2. Add the minced pork to the skillet. Using a spoon, break the pork into smaller chunks. 3. In a small bowl, whisk the sesame oil, soy sauce, and ginger until combined. Add the sauce to the skillet. Stir to combine and continue cooking for about 5 minutes until the pork is browned and thoroughly cooked. 4. Stir in the cabbage and spring onions. Transfer the pork mixture to a large bowl. 5. Lay the egg roll wrappers on a flat surface. Dip a basting brush in water and glaze each egg roll wrapper along the edges with the wet brush. This will soften the dough and make it easier to roll. 6. Stack 2 egg roll wrappers (it works best if you double-wrap the egg rolls). Scoop 1 to 2 tablespoons of the pork mixture into the centre of each wrapper stack. 7. Roll one long side of the wrappers up over the filling. Press firmly on the area with the filling, tucking it in lightly to secure it in place. Fold in the left and right sides. Continue rolling to close. Use the basting brush to wet the seam and seal the egg roll. Repeat with the remaining ingredients. 8. Insert the crisper plate into the basket and the basket into the unit. Preheat the unit by selecting AIR FRY, setting the temperature to 204°C, and setting the time to 3 minutes. Select START/STOP to begin. 9. Once the unit is preheated, spray the crisper plate with cooking oil. Place the egg rolls into the basket. It is okay to stack them. Spray them with cooking oil. 10. Select AIR FRY, set the temperature to 204°C, and set the time to 12 minutes. Insert the basket into the unit. Select START/STOP to begin. 11. After 8 minutes, use tongs to flip the egg rolls. Reinsert the basket to resume cooking. 12. When the cooking is complete, serve the egg rolls hot.

Italian Rice Balls

Prep time: 20 minutes | Cook time: 10 minutes | Makes 8 rice balls

355 ml cooked sticky rice
½ teaspoon Italian seasoning blend
¾ teaspoon salt, divided
8 black olives, pitted
28 g Mozzarella cheese, cut

into tiny pieces (small enough to stuff into olives)
2 eggs
80 ml Italian breadcrumbs
177 ml panko breadcrumbs
Cooking spray

1. Preheat air fryer to 200°C. 2. Stuff each black olive with a piece of Mozzarella cheese. Set aside. 3. In a bowl, combine the cooked sticky rice, Italian seasoning blend, and ½ teaspoon of salt and stir to mix well. Form the rice mixture into a log with your hands and divide it into 8 equal portions. Mould each portion around a black olive and roll into a ball. 4. Transfer to the freezer to chill for 10 to 15 minutes until firm. 5. In a shallow dish, place the Italian breadcrumbs. In a separate shallow dish, whisk the eggs. In a third shallow dish, combine the panko breadcrumbs and remaining salt. 6. One by one, roll the rice balls in the Italian breadcrumbs, then dip in the whisked eggs, finally coat them with the panko breadcrumbs. 7. Arrange the rice balls in the air fryer basket and spritz both sides with cooking spray. 8. Air fry for 10 minutes until the rice balls are golden brown. Flip the balls halfway through the cooking time. 9. Serve warm.

Spicy Chicken Bites

Prep time: 10 minutes | Cook time: 10 to 12 minutes | Makes 30 bites

227 g boneless and skinless chicken thighs, cut into 30 pieces

¼ teaspoon rock salt
2 tablespoons hot sauce
Cooking spray

1. Preheat the air fryer to 200°C. 2. Spray the air fryer basket with cooking spray and season the chicken bites with the rock salt, then place in the basket and air fry for 10 to 12 minutes or until crispy. 3. While the chicken bites cook, pour the hot sauce into a large bowl. 4. Remove the bites and add to the sauce bowl, tossing to coat. Serve warm.

Crispy Breaded Beef Cubes

Prep time: 10 minutes | Cook time: 12 to 16 minutes | Serves 4

450 g sirloin tip, cut into 1-inch cubes
240 ml cheese pasta sauce

355 ml soft breadcrumbs
2 tablespoons olive oil
½ teaspoon dried marjoram

1. Preheat the air fryer to 182°C. 2. In a medium bowl, toss the beef with the pasta sauce to coat. 3. In a shallow bowl, combine the breadcrumbs, oil, and marjoram, and mix well. Drop the beef cubes, one at a time, into the bread crumb mixture to coat thoroughly. 4. Air fry the beef in two batches for 6 to 8 minutes, shaking the basket once during cooking time, until the beef is at least 63°C and the outside is crisp and brown. 5. Serve hot.

Mexican Potato Skins

Prep time: 10 minutes | Cook time: 55 minutes | Serves 6

Olive oil
6 medium russet or Maris Piper potatoes, scrubbed
Salt and freshly ground black pepper, to taste
240 ml fat-free refried black

beans
1 tablespoon taco seasoning
120 ml salsa
177 ml low-fat shredded Cheddar cheese

1. Spray the air fryer basket lightly with olive oil. 2. Spray the potatoes lightly with oil and season with salt and pepper. Pierce each potato a few times with a fork. 3. Place the potatoes in the air fryer basket. Air fry at 204°C until fork-tender, 30 to 40 minutes. The cooking time will depend on the size of the potatoes. You can cook the potatoes in the microwave or a standard oven, but they won't get the same lovely crispy skin they will get in the air fryer. 4. While the potatoes are cooking, in a small bowl, mix together the beans and taco seasoning. Set aside until the potatoes are cool

enough to handle. 5. Cut each potato in half lengthwise. Scoop out most of the insides, leaving about ¼ inch in the skins so the potato skins hold their shape. 6. Season the insides of the potato skins with salt and black pepper. Lightly spray the insides of the potato skins with oil. You may need to cook them in batches. 7. Place them into the air fryer basket, skin-side down, and air fry until crisp and golden, 8 to 10 minutes. 8. Transfer the skins to a work surface and spoon ½ tablespoon of seasoned refried black beans into each one. Top each with 2 teaspoons salsa and 1 tablespoon shredded Cheddar cheese. 9. Place filled potato skins in the air fryer basket in a single layer. Lightly spray with oil. 10. Air fry until the cheese is melted and bubbly, 2 to 3 minutes.

Stuffed Figs with Goat Cheese and Honey

Prep time: 5 minutes | Cook time: 10 minutes | Serves 4

8 fresh figs
57 g goat cheese
¼ teaspoon ground cinnamon

1 tablespoon honey, plus more for serving
1 tablespoon olive oil

1. Preheat the air fryer to 182°C. Line an 8-by-8-inch baking dish with parchment paper that comes up the side so you can lift it out after cooking. 2. In a large bowl, mix together all of the ingredients until well combined. 3. Press the oat mixture into the pan in an even layer. 4. Place the pan into the air fryer basket and bake for 15 minutes. 5. Remove the pan from the air fryer and lift the granola cake out of the pan using the edges of the parchment paper. 6. Allow to cool for 5 minutes before slicing into 6 equal bars. 7. Serve immediately or wrap in plastic wrap and store at room temperature for up to 1 week.

Peppery Chicken Meatballs

Prep time: 5 minutes | Cook time: 13 to 20 minutes | Makes 16 meatballs

2 teaspoons olive oil
60 ml minced onion
60 ml minced red pepper
2 vanilla wafers, crushed

1 egg white
½ teaspoon dried thyme
230 g minced chicken breast

1. Preheat the air fryer to 188°C. 2. In a baking pan, mix the olive oil, onion, and red pepper. Put the pan in the air fryer. Air fry for 3 to 5 minutes, or until the vegetables are tender. 3. In a medium bowl, mix the cooked vegetables, crushed wafers, egg white, and thyme until well combined 4. Mix in the chicken, gently but thoroughly, until everything is combined. 5. Form the mixture into 16 meatballs and place them in the air fryer basket. Air fry for 10 to 15 minutes, or until the meatballs reach an internal temperature of 74°C on a meat thermometer. 6. Serve immediately.

Pickle Chips

Prep time: 30 minutes | Cook time: 12 minutes | Serves 4

Oil, for spraying
475 ml sliced dill or sweet
pickles, drained
240 ml buttermilk

475 ml plain flour
2 large eggs, beaten
475 ml panko breadcrumbs
¼ teaspoon salt

1. Line the air fryer basket with parchment and spray lightly with oil. 2. In a shallow bowl, combine the pickles and buttermilk and let soak for at least 1 hour, then drain. 3. Place the flour, beaten eggs, and breadcrumbs in separate bowls. 4. Coat each pickle chip lightly in the flour, dip in the eggs, and dredge in the breadcrumbs. Be sure each one is evenly coated. 5. Place the pickle chips in the prepared basket, sprinkle with the salt, and spray lightly with oil. You may need to work in batches, depending on the size of your air fryer. 6. Air fry at 200ºC for 5 minutes, flip, and cook for another 5 to 7 minutes, or until crispy. Serve hot.

Sea Salt Potato Crisps

Prep time: 30 minutes | Cook time: 27 minutes | Serves 4

Oil, for spraying
4 medium yellow potatoes such
as Maris Pipers

1 tablespoon oil
⅛ to ¼ teaspoon fine sea salt

1. Line the air fryer basket with parchment and spray lightly with oil. 2. Using a mandoline or a very sharp knife, cut the potatoes into very thin slices. 3. Place the slices in a bowl of cold water and let soak for about 20 minutes. 4. Drain the potatoes, transfer them to a plate lined with paper towels, and pat dry. 5. Drizzle the oil over the potatoes, sprinkle with the salt, and toss to combine. Transfer to the prepared basket. 6. Air fry at 92ºC for 20 minutes. Toss the crisps, increase the heat to 204ºC, and cook for another 5 to 7 minutes, until crispy.

Chilli-Brined Fried Calamari

Prep time: 20 minutes | Cook time: 8 minutes | Serves 2

1 (227 g) jar sweet or hot
pickled cherry peppers
227 g calamari bodies and
tentacles, bodies cut into
½-inch-wide rings
1 lemon
475 ml plain flour
Rock salt and freshly ground

black pepper, to taste
3 large eggs, lightly beaten
Cooking spray
120 ml mayonnaise
1 teaspoon finely chopped
rosemary
1 garlic clove, minced

1. Drain the pickled pepper brine into a large bowl and tear the peppers into bite-size strips. Add the pepper strips and calamari to the brine and let stand in the refrigerator for 20 minutes or up

to 2 hours. 2. Grate the lemon zest into a large bowl then whisk in the flour and season with salt and pepper. Dip the calamari and pepper strips in the egg, then toss them in the flour mixture until fully coated. Spray the calamari and peppers liberally with cooking spray, then transfer half to the air fryer. Air fry at 204ºC, shaking the basket halfway into cooking, until the calamari is cooked through and golden brown, about 8 minutes. Transfer to a plate and repeat with the remaining pieces. 3. In a small bowl, whisk together the mayonnaise, rosemary, and garlic. Squeeze half the zested lemon to get 1 tablespoon of juice and stir it into the sauce. Season with salt and pepper. Cut the remaining zested lemon half into 4 small wedges and serve alongside the calamari, peppers, and sauce.

Jalapeño Poppers

Prep time: 10 minutes | Cook time: 20 minutes | Serves 4

Oil, for spraying
227 g soft white cheese
177 ml gluten-free
breadcrumbs, divided
2 tablespoons chopped fresh

parsley
½ teaspoon granulated garlic
½ teaspoon salt
10 jalapeño peppers, halved and
seeded

1. Line the air fryer basket with parchment and spray lightly with oil. 2. In a medium bowl, mix together the soft white cheese, half of the breadcrumbs, the parsley, garlic, and salt. 3. Spoon the mixture into the jalapeño halves. Gently press the stuffed jalapeños in the remaining breadcrumbs. 4. Place the stuffed jalapeños in the prepared basket. 5. Air fry at 188ºC for 20 minutes, or until the cheese is melted and the breadcrumbs are crisp and golden brown.

Fried Artichoke Hearts

**Prep time: 10 minutes | Cook time: 12 minutes |
Serves 10**

Oil, for spraying
3 (397 g) cans quartered
artichokes, drained and patted
dry
120 ml mayonnaise

240 ml panko breadcrumbs
80 ml grated Parmesan cheese
Salt and freshly ground black
pepper, to taste

1. Line the air fryer basket with parchment and spray lightly with oil. 2. Place the artichokes on a plate. Put the mayonnaise and breadcrumbs in separate bowls. 3. Working one at a time, dredge each artichoke piece in the mayonnaise, then in the breadcrumbs to cover. 4. Place the artichokes in the prepared basket. You may need to work in batches, depending on the size of your air fryer. 5. Air fry at 188ºC for 10 to 12 minutes, or until crispy and golden brown. 6. Sprinkle with the Parmesan cheese and season with salt and black pepper. Serve immediately.

Lemon Shrimp with Garlic Olive Oil

Prep time: 5 minutes | Cook time: 6 minutes | Serves 4

454 g medium shrimp, cleaned and deveined
60 ml plus 2 tablespoons olive oil, divided
Juice of ½ lemon
3 garlic cloves, minced and divided

½ teaspoon salt
¼ teaspoon red pepper flakes
Lemon wedges, for serving (optional)
Marinara sauce, for dipping (optional)

1. Preheat the air fryer to 192°C. 2. In a large bowl, combine the shrimp with 2 tablespoons of the olive oil, as well as the lemon juice, ⅓ of the minced garlic, salt, and red pepper flakes. Toss to coat the shrimp well. 3. In a small ramekin, combine the remaining 60 ml of olive oil and the remaining minced garlic. 4. Tear off a 12-by-12-inch sheet of aluminium foil. Pour the shrimp into the centre of the foil, then fold the sides up and crimp the edges so that it forms an aluminium foil bowl that is open on top. Place this packet into the air fryer basket. 5. Roast the shrimp for 4 minutes, then open the air fryer and place the ramekin with oil and garlic in the basket beside the shrimp packet. Cook for 2 more minutes. 6. Transfer the shrimp on a serving plate or platter with the ramekin of garlic olive oil on the side for dipping. You may also serve with lemon wedges and marinara sauce, if desired.

Vegetable Pot Stickers

Prep time: 12 minutes | Cook time: 11 to 18 minutes | Makes 12 pot stickers

240 ml shredded red cabbage
60 ml chopped button mushrooms
60 ml grated carrot
2 tablespoons minced onion

2 garlic cloves, minced
2 teaspoons grated fresh ginger
12 gyoza/pot sticker wrappers
2½ teaspoons olive oil, divided

1. In a baking pan, combine the red cabbage, mushrooms, carrot, onion, garlic, and ginger. Add 1 tablespoon of water. Place in the air fryer and air fry at 188°C for 3 to 6 minutes, until the vegetables are crisp-tender. Drain and set aside. 2. Working one at a time, place the pot sticker wrappers on a work surface. Top each wrapper with a scant 1 tablespoon of the filling. Fold half of the wrapper over the other half to form a half circle. Dab one edge with water and press both edges together. 3. To another pan, add 1¼ teaspoons of olive oil. Put half of the pot stickers, seam-side up, in the pan. Air fry for 5 minutes, or until the bottoms are light golden brown. Add 1 tablespoon of water and return the pan to the air fryer. 4. Air fry for 4 to 6 minutes more, or until hot. Repeat with the remaining pot stickers, remaining 1¼ teaspoons of oil, and another tablespoon of water. Serve immediately.

Honey-Mustard Chicken Wings

Prep time: 10 minutes | Cook time: 24 minutes | Serves 2

907 g chicken wings
Salt and freshly ground black pepper, to taste
2 tablespoons butter
60 ml honey

60 ml spicy brown mustard
Pinch ground cayenne pepper
2 teaspoons Worcestershire sauce

1. Prepare the chicken wings by cutting off the wing tips and discarding (or freezing for chicken stock). Divide the drumettes from the wingettes by cutting through the joint. Place the chicken wing pieces in a large bowl. 2. Preheat the air fryer to 204°C. 3. Season the wings with salt and freshly ground black pepper and air fry the wings in two batches for 10 minutes per batch, shaking the basket halfway through the cooking process. 4. While the wings are air frying, combine the remaining ingredients in a small saucepan over low heat. 5. When both batches are done, toss all the wings with the honey-mustard sauce and toss them all back into the basket for another 4 minutes to heat through and finish cooking. Give the basket a good shake part way through the cooking process to redistribute the wings. Remove the wings from the air fryer and serve.

Crispy Green Bean Fries with Lemon-Yoghurt Sauce

Prep time: 5 minutes | Cook time: 5 minutes | Serves 4

Green Beans:
1 egg
2 tablespoons water
1 tablespoon wholemeal flour
¼ teaspoon paprika
½ teaspoon garlic powder
½ teaspoon salt
60 ml wholemeal breadcrumbs

227 g whole green beans
Lemon-Yoghurt Sauce:
120 ml non-fat plain Greek yoghurt
1 tablespoon lemon juice
¼ teaspoon salt
⅛ teaspoon cayenne pepper

Make the Green Beans: 1. Preheat the air fryer to 192°C. 2. In a medium shallow bowl, beat together the egg and water until frothy. 3. In a separate medium shallow bowl, whisk together the flour, paprika, garlic powder, and salt, then mix in the breadcrumbs. 4. Spray the bottom of the air fryer with cooking spray. 5. Dip each green bean into the egg mixture, then into the bread crumb mixture, coating the outside with the crumbs. Place the green beans in a single layer in the bottom of the air fryer basket. 6. Fry in the air fryer for 5 minutes, or until the breading is golden brown. Make the Lemon-Yoghurt Sauce: 7. In a small bowl, combine the yoghurt, lemon juice, salt, and cayenne. 8. Serve the green bean fries alongside the lemon-yoghurt sauce as a snack or appetizer.

Spinach and Crab Meat Cups

Prep time: 10 minutes | Cook time: 10 minutes | Makes 30 cups

1 (170 g) can crab meat, drained to yield 80 ml meat
60 ml frozen spinach, thawed, drained, and chopped
1 clove garlic, minced
120 ml grated Parmesan cheese
3 tablespoons plain yoghurt
¼ teaspoon lemon juice
½ teaspoon Worcestershire sauce
30 mini frozen filo shells, thawed
Cooking spray

1. Preheat the air fryer to 200ºC. 2. Remove any bits of shell that might remain in the crab meat. 3. Mix the crab meat, spinach, garlic, and cheese together. 4. Stir in the yoghurt, lemon juice, and Worcestershire sauce and mix well. 5. Spoon a teaspoon of filling into each filo shell. 6. Spray the air fryer basket with cooking spray and arrange half the shells in the basket. Air fry for 5 minutes. Repeat with the remaining shells. 7. Serve immediately.

Skinny Fries

Prep time: 10 minutes | Cook time: 15 minutes per batch | Serves 2

2 to 3 russet or Maris Piper potatoes, peeled and cut into ¼-inch sticks
2 to 3 teaspoons olive or vegetable oil
Salt, to taste

1. Cut the potatoes into ¼-inch strips. (A mandolin with a julienne blade is really helpful here.) Rinse the potatoes with cold water several times and let them soak in cold water for at least 10 minutes or as long as overnight. 2. Preheat the air fryer to 192ºC. 3. Drain and dry the potato sticks really well, using a clean kitchen towel. Toss the fries with the oil in a bowl and then air fry the fries in two batches at 192ºC for 15 minutes, shaking the basket a couple of times while they cook. 4. Add the first batch of French fries back into the air fryer basket with the finishing batch and let everything warm through for a few minutes. As soon as the fries are done, season them with salt and transfer to a plate or basket. Serve them warm with ketchup or your favourite dip.

Garlic Edamame

Prep time: 5 minutes | Cook time: 10 minutes | Serves 4

Olive oil
1 (454 g) bag frozen edamame in pods
½ teaspoon salt
½ teaspoon garlic salt
¼ teaspoon freshly ground black pepper
½ teaspoon red pepper flakes (optional)

1. Spray the air fryer basket lightly with olive oil. 2. In a medium bowl, add the frozen edamame and lightly spray with olive oil. Toss to coat. 3. In a small bowl, mix together the salt, garlic salt, black pepper, and red pepper flakes (if using). Add the mixture to the edamame and toss until evenly coated. 4. Place half the edamame in the air fryer basket. Do not overfill the basket. 5. Air fry at 192ºC for 5 minutes. Shake the basket and cook until the edamame is starting to brown and get crispy, 3 to 5 more minutes. 6. Repeat with the remaining edamame and serve immediately.

String Bean Fries

Prep time: 15 minutes | Cook time: 5 to 6 minutes | Serves 4

227 g fresh green beans
2 eggs
4 teaspoons water
120 ml white flour
120 ml breadcrumbs
¼ teaspoon salt
¼ teaspoon ground black pepper
¼ teaspoon mustard powder (optional)
Oil for misting or cooking spray

1. Preheat the air fryer to 182ºC. 2. Trim stem ends from green beans, wash, and pat dry. 3. In a shallow dish, beat eggs and water together until well blended. 4. Place flour in a second shallow dish. 5. In a third shallow dish, stir together the breadcrumbs, salt, pepper, and dry mustard if using. 6. Dip each bean in egg mixture, flour, egg mixture again, then breadcrumbs. 7. When you finish coating all the green beans, open air fryer and place them in basket. 8. Cook for 3 minutes. 9. Stop and mist green beans with oil or cooking spray. 10. Cook for 2 to 3 more minutes or until green beans are crispy and nicely browned.

Chapter 3 Beef, Pork, and Lamb

Cheesy Low-Carb Lasagna

Prep time: 10 minutes | Cook time: 10 minutes | Serves 4

Meat Layer:
Extra-virgin olive oil
450 g 85% lean beef mince
235 ml marinara sauce
60 ml diced celery
60 ml diced red onion
½ teaspoon minced garlic
Coarse or flaky salt and black pepper, to taste
Cheese Layer:

230 g ricotta cheese
235 ml shredded Mozzarella cheese
120 ml grated Parmesan cheese
2 large eggs
1 teaspoon dried Italian seasoning, crushed
½ teaspoon each minced garlic, garlic powder, and black pepper

1. For the meat layer: Grease a cake pan with 1 teaspoon olive oil. 2. In a large bowl, combine the beef mince, marinara, celery, onion, garlic, salt, and pepper. Place the seasoned meat in the pan. 3. Place the pan in the air fryer basket. Set the air fryer to 192°C for 10 minutes. 4. Meanwhile, for the cheese layer: In a medium bowl, combine the ricotta, half the Mozzarella, the Parmesan, lightly beaten eggs, Italian seasoning, minced garlic, garlic powder, and pepper. Stir until well blended. 5. At the end of the cooking time, spread the cheese mixture over the meat mixture. Sprinkle with the remaining 120 ml Mozzarella. Set the air fryer to 192°C for 10 minutes, or until the cheese is browned and bubbling. 6. At the end of the cooking time, use a meat thermometer to ensure the meat has reached an internal temperature of 72°C. 7. Drain the fat and liquid from the pan. Let stand for 5 minutes before serving.

Steak with Bell Pepper

Prep time: 30 minutes | Cook time: 20 to 23 minutes | Serves 6

60 ml avocado oil
60 ml freshly squeezed lime juice
2 teaspoons minced garlic
1 tablespoon chili powder
½ teaspoon ground cumin
Sea salt and freshly ground black pepper, to taste

450 g top rump steak or bavette or skirt steak, thinly sliced against the grain
1 red pepper, cored, seeded, and cut into ½-inch slices
1 green pepper, cored, seeded, and cut into ½-inch slices
1 large onion, sliced

1. In a small bowl or blender, combine the avocado oil, lime juice, garlic, chili powder, cumin, and salt and pepper to taste. 2. Place the sliced steak in a zip-top bag or shallow dish. Place the peppers and onion in a separate zip-top bag or dish. Pour half the marinade over the steak and the other half over the vegetables. Seal both bags and let the steak and vegetables marinate in the refrigerator for at least 1 hour or up to 4 hours. 3. Line the air fryer basket with an air fryer liner or aluminum foil. Remove the vegetables from their bag or dish and shake off any excess marinade. Set the air fryer to 204°C. Place the vegetables in the air fryer basket and cook for 13 minutes. 4. Remove the steak from its bag or dish and shake off any excess marinade. Place the steak on top of the vegetables in the air fryer, and cook for 7 to 10 minutes or until an instant-read thermometer reads 49°C for medium-rare (or cook to your desired doneness). 5. Serve with desired fixings, such as keto tortillas, lettuce, sour cream, avocado slices, shredded Cheddar cheese, and coriander.

Pork and Beef Egg Rolls

Prep time: 30 minutes | Cook time: 7 to 8 minutes per batch | Makes 8 egg rolls

110 g very lean beef mince
110 g lean pork mince
1 tablespoon soy sauce
1 teaspoon olive oil
120 ml grated carrots
2 green onions, chopped
475 ml grated Chinese cabbage
60 ml chopped water chestnuts

¼ teaspoon salt
¼ teaspoon garlic powder
¼ teaspoon black pepper
1 egg
1 tablespoon water
8 egg roll wrappers
Oil for misting or cooking spray

1. In a large skillet, brown beef and pork with soy sauce. Remove cooked meat from skillet, drain, and set aside. 2. Pour off any excess grease from skillet. Add olive oil, carrots, and onions. Sauté until barely tender, about 1 minute. 3. Stir in cabbage, cover, and cook for 1 minute or just until cabbage slightly wilts. Remove from heat. 4. In a large bowl, combine the cooked meats and vegetables, water chestnuts, salt, garlic powder, and pepper. Stir well. If needed, add more salt to taste. 5. Beat together egg and water in a small bowl. 6. Fill egg roll wrappers, using about 60 ml of filling for each wrap. Roll up and brush all over with egg wash to seal. Spray very lightly with olive oil or cooking spray. 7. Place 4 egg rolls in air fryer basket and air fry at 200°C for 4 minutes. Turn over and cook 3 to 4 more minutes, until golden brown and crispy. 8. Repeat to cook remaining egg rolls.

Swedish Meatloaf

Prep time: 10 minutes | Cook time: 35 minutes | Serves 8

680 g beef mince (85% lean)
110 g pork mince
1 large egg (omit for egg-free)
120 ml minced onions
60 ml tomato sauce
2 tablespoons mustard powder
2 cloves garlic, minced
2 teaspoons fine sea salt
1 teaspoon ground black pepper, plus more for garnish

Sauce:
120 ml (1 stick) unsalted butter
120 ml shredded Swiss or mild Cheddar cheese (about 60 g)
60 g cream cheese (60 ml), softened
80 ml beef stock
⅛ teaspoon ground nutmeg
Halved cherry tomatoes, for serving (optional)

1. Preheat the air fryer to 200°C. 2. In a large bowl, combine the beef, pork, egg, onions, tomato sauce, mustard powder, garlic, salt, and pepper. Using your hands, mix until well combined. 3. Place the meatloaf mixture in a loaf pan and place it in the air fryer. Bake for 35 minutes, or until cooked through and the internal temperature reaches 64°C. Check the meatloaf after 25 minutes; if it's getting too brown on the top, cover it loosely with foil to prevent burning. 4. While the meatloaf cooks, make the sauce: Heat the butter in a saucepan over medium-high heat until it sizzles and brown flecks appear, stirring constantly to keep the butter from burning. Turn the heat down to low and whisk in the Swiss cheese, cream cheese, stock, and nutmeg. Simmer for at least 10 minutes. The longer it simmers, the more the flavors open up. 5. When the meatloaf is done, transfer it to a serving tray and pour the sauce over it. Garnish with ground black pepper and serve with cherry tomatoes, if desired. Allow the meatloaf to rest for 10 minutes before slicing so it doesn't crumble apart. 6. Store leftovers in an airtight container in the fridge for 3 days or in the freezer for up to a month. Reheat in a preheated 176°C air fryer for 4 minutes, or until heated through.

Bacon-Wrapped Vegetable Kebabs

Prep time: 10 minutes | Cook time: 10 to 12 minutes | Serves 4

110 g mushrooms, sliced
1 small courgette, sliced
12 baby plum tomatoes
110 g sliced bacon, halved

Avocado oil spray
Sea salt and freshly ground black pepper, to taste

1. Stack 3 mushroom slices, 1 courgette slice, and 1 tomato. Wrap a bacon strip around the vegetables and thread them onto a skewer. Repeat with the remaining vegetables and bacon. Spray with oil and sprinkle with salt and pepper. 2. Set the air fryer to 204°C. Place the skewers in the air fryer basket in a single layer, working in batches if necessary, and air fry for 5 minutes. Flip the skewers and cook for 5 to 7 minutes more, until the bacon is crispy and the vegetables are tender. 3. Serve warm.

Kheema Burgers

Prep time: 15 minutes | Cook time: 12 minutes | Serves 4

Burgers:
450 g 85% lean beef mince or lamb mince
2 large eggs, lightly beaten
1 medium brown onion, diced
60 ml chopped fresh coriander
1 tablespoon minced fresh ginger
3 cloves garlic, minced
2 teaspoons garam masala
1 teaspoon ground turmeric
½ teaspoon ground cinnamon

⅛ teaspoon ground cardamom
1 teaspoon coarse or flaky salt
1 teaspoon cayenne pepper
Raita Sauce:
235 ml grated cucumber
120 ml sour cream
¼ teaspoon coarse or flaky salt
¼ teaspoon black pepper
For Serving:
4 lettuce leaves, hamburger buns, or naan breads

1. For the burgers: In a large bowl, combine the beef mince, eggs, onion, coriander, ginger, garlic, garam masala, turmeric, cinnamon, cardamom, salt, and cayenne. Gently mix until ingredients are thoroughly combined. 2. Divide the meat into four portions and form into round patties. Make a slight depression in the middle of each patty with your thumb to prevent them from puffing up into a dome shape while cooking. 3. Place the patties in the air fryer basket. Set the air fryer to 176°C for 12 minutes. Use a meat thermometer to ensure the burgers have reached an internal temperature of 72°C (for medium). 4. Meanwhile, for the sauce: In a small bowl, combine the cucumber, sour cream, salt, and pepper. 5. To serve: Place the burgers on the lettuce, buns, or naan and top with the sauce.

Stuffed Beef Fillet with Feta Cheese

Prep time: 10 minutes | Cook time: 10 minutes | Serves 4

680 g beef fillet, pounded to ¼ inch thick
3 teaspoons sea salt
1 teaspoon ground black pepper
60 g creamy goat cheese

120 ml crumbled feta cheese
60 ml finely chopped onions
2 cloves garlic, minced
Cooking spray

1. Preheat the air fryer to 204°C. Spritz the air fryer basket with cooking spray. 2. Unfold the beef on a clean work surface. Rub the salt and pepper all over the beef to season. 3. Make the filling for the stuffed beef fillet: Combine the goat cheese, feta, onions, and garlic in a medium bowl. Stir until well blended. 4. Spoon the mixture in the center of the fillet. Roll the fillet up tightly like rolling a burrito and use some kitchen twine to tie the fillet. 5. Arrange the fillet in the air fryer basket and air fry for 10 minutes, flipping the fillet halfway through to ensure even cooking, or until an instant-read thermometer inserted in the center of the fillet registers 57°C for medium-rare. 6. Transfer to a platter and serve immediately.

Italian Sausages with Peppers and Onions

Prep time: 5 minutes | Cook time: 28 minutes | Serves 3

1 medium onion, thinly sliced	coconut oil
1 yellow or orange pepper, thinly sliced	1 teaspoon fine sea salt
1 red pepper, thinly sliced	6 Italian-seasoned sausages
60 ml avocado oil or melted	Dijon mustard, for serving (optional)

1. Preheat the air fryer to 204ºC. 2. Place the onion and peppers in a large bowl. Drizzle with the oil and toss well to coat the veggies. Season with the salt. 3. Place the onion and peppers in a pie pan and cook in the air fryer for 8 minutes, stirring halfway through. Remove from the air fryer and set aside. 4. Spray the air fryer basket with avocado oil. Place the sausages in the air fryer basket and air fry for 20 minutes, or until crispy and golden brown. During the last minute or two of cooking, add the onion and peppers to the basket with the sausages to warm them through. 5. Place the onion and peppers on a serving platter and arrange the sausages on top. Serve Dijon mustard on the side, if desired. 6. Store leftovers in an airtight container in the fridge for up to 7 days or in the freezer for up to a month. Reheat in a preheated 200ºC air fryer for 3 minutes, or until heated through.

Pork Shoulder with Garlicky Coriander-Parsley Sauce

Prep time: 1 hour 15 minutes | Cook time: 30 minutes | Serves 4

1 teaspoon flaxseed meal	to taste
1 egg white, well whisked	Garlicky Coriander-Parsley Sauce:
1 tablespoon soy sauce	3 garlic cloves, minced
1 teaspoon lemon juice, preferably freshly squeezed	80 ml fresh coriander leaves
1 tablespoon olive oil	80 ml fresh parsley leaves
450 g pork shoulder, cut into pieces 2-inches long	1 teaspoon lemon juice
Salt and ground black pepper,	½ tablespoon salt
	80 ml extra-virgin olive oil

1. Combine the flaxseed meal, egg white, soy sauce, lemon juice, salt, black pepper, and olive oil in a large bowl. Dunk the pork strips in and press to submerge. 2. Wrap the bowl in plastic and refrigerate to marinate for at least an hour. 3. Preheat the air fryer to 192ºC. 4. Arrange the marinated pork strips in the preheated air fryer and air fry for 30 minutes or until cooked through and well browned. Flip the strips halfway through. 5. Meanwhile, combine the ingredients for the sauce in a small bowl. Stir to mix well. Arrange the bowl in the refrigerator to chill until ready to serve. 6. Serve the air fried pork strips with the chilled sauce.

Short Ribs with Chimichurri

Prep time: 30 minutes | Cook time: 13 minutes | Serves 4

450 g boneless short ribs	1 tablespoon freshly squeezed lemon juice
1½ teaspoons sea salt, divided	½ teaspoon ground cumin
½ teaspoon freshly ground black pepper, divided	¼ teaspoon red pepper flakes
120 ml fresh parsley leaves	2 tablespoons extra-virgin olive oil
120 ml fresh coriander leaves	Avocado oil spray
1 teaspoon minced garlic	

1. Pat the short ribs dry with paper towels. Sprinkle the ribs all over with 1 teaspoon salt and ¼ teaspoon black pepper. Let sit at room temperature for 45 minutes. 2. Meanwhile, place the parsley, coriander, garlic, lemon juice, cumin, red pepper flakes, the remaining ½ teaspoon salt, and the remaining ¼ teaspoon black pepper in a blender or food processor. With the blender running, slowly drizzle in the olive oil. Blend for about 1 minute, until the mixture is smooth and well combined. 3. Set the air fryer to 204ºC. Spray both sides of the ribs with oil. Place in the basket and air fry for 8 minutes. Flip and cook for another 5 minutes, until an instant-read thermometer reads 52ºC for medium-rare (or to your desired doneness). 4. Allow the meat to rest for 5 to 10 minutes, then slice. Serve warm with the chimichurri sauce.

London Broil with Herb Butter

Prep time: 30 minutes | Cook time: 20 to 25 minutes | Serves 4

680 g bavette or skirt steak	softened
60 ml olive oil	1 tablespoon chopped fresh parsley
2 tablespoons balsamic vinegar	¼ teaspoon salt
1 tablespoon Worcestershire sauce	¼ teaspoon dried ground rosemary or thyme
4 cloves garlic, minced	¼ teaspoon garlic powder
Herb Butter:	Pinch of red pepper flakes
6 tablespoons unsalted butter,	

1. Place the beef in a gallon-size resealable bag. In a small bowl, whisk together the olive oil, balsamic vinegar, Worcestershire sauce, and garlic. Pour the marinade over the beef, massaging gently to coat, and seal the bag. Let sit at room temperature for an hour or refrigerate overnight. 2. To make the herb butter: In a small bowl, mix the butter with the parsley, salt, rosemary, garlic powder, and red pepper flakes until smooth. Cover and refrigerate until ready to use. 3. Preheat the air fryer to 204ºC. 4. Remove the beef from the marinade (discard the marinade) and place the beef in the air fryer basket. Pausing halfway through the cooking time to turn the meat, air fry for 20 to 25 minutes, until a thermometer inserted into the thickest part indicates the desired doneness, 52ºC (rare) to 64ºC (medium). Let the beef rest for 10 minutes before slicing. Serve topped with the herb butter.

Fillet with Crispy Shallots

Prep time: 30 minutes | Cook time: 18 to 20 minutes | Serves 6

680 g beef fillet steaks	4 medium shallots
Sea salt and freshly ground black pepper, to taste	1 teaspoon olive oil or avocado oil

1. Season both sides of the steaks with salt and pepper, and let them sit at room temperature for 45 minutes. 2. Set the air fryer to 204ºC and let it preheat for 5 minutes. 3. Working in batches if necessary, place the steaks in the air fryer basket in a single layer and air fry for 5 minutes. Flip and cook for 5 minutes longer, until an instant-read thermometer inserted in the center of the steaks registers 49ºC for medium-rare (or as desired). Remove the steaks and tent with aluminum foil to rest. 4. Set the air fryer to 149ºC. In a medium bowl, toss the shallots with the oil. Place the shallots in the basket and air fry for 5 minutes, then give them a toss and cook for 3 to 5 minutes more, until crispy and golden brown. 5. Place the steaks on serving plates and arrange the shallots on top.

Kale and Beef Omelet

Prep time: 15 minutes | Cook time: 16 minutes | Serves 4

230 g leftover beef, coarsely chopped	4 eggs, beaten
2 garlic cloves, pressed	4 tablespoons double cream
235 ml kale, torn into pieces and wilted	½ teaspoon turmeric powder
1 tomato, chopped	Salt and ground black pepper, to taste
¼ teaspoon sugar	⅛ teaspoon ground allspice
	Cooking spray

1. Preheat the air fryer to 182ºC. Spritz four ramekins with cooking spray. 2. Put equal amounts of each of the ingredients into each ramekin and mix well. 3. Air fry for 16 minutes. Serve immediately.

Mojito Lamb Chops

Prep time: 30 minutes | Cook time: 5 minutes | Serves 2

Marinade:	2 teaspoons fine sea salt
2 teaspoons grated lime zest	½ teaspoon ground black pepper
120 ml lime juice	
60 ml avocado oil	4 (1-inch-thick) lamb chops
60 ml chopped fresh mint leaves	Sprigs of fresh mint, for garnish (optional)
4 cloves garlic, roughly chopped	Lime slices, for serving (optional)

1. Make the marinade: Place all the ingredients for the marinade in a food processor or blender and purée until mostly smooth with a few small chunks. Transfer half of the marinade to a shallow dish and set the other half aside for serving. Add the lamb to the shallow dish, cover, and place in the refrigerator to marinate for at least 2 hours or overnight. 2. Spray the air fryer basket with avocado oil. Preheat the air fryer to 200ºC. 3. Remove the chops from the marinade and place them in the air fryer basket. Air fry for 5 minutes, or until the internal temperature reaches 64ºC for medium doneness. 4. Allow the chops to rest for 10 minutes before serving with the rest of the marinade as a sauce. Garnish with fresh mint leaves and serve with lime slices, if desired. Best served fresh.

Bacon-Wrapped Hot Dogs with Mayo-Ketchup Sauce

Prep time: 5 minutes | Cook time: 10 to 12 minutes | Serves 5

10 thin slices of bacon	60 ml mayonnaise
5 pork hot dogs, halved	4 tablespoons ketchup
1 teaspoon cayenne pepper	1 teaspoon rice vinegar
Sauce:	1 teaspoon chili powder

1. Preheat the air fryer to 200ºC. 2. Arrange the slices of bacon on a clean work surface. One by one, place the halved hot dog on one end of each slice, season with cayenne pepper and wrap the hot dog with the bacon slices and secure with toothpicks as needed. 3. Work in batches, place half the wrapped hot dogs in the air fryer basket and air fry for 10 to 12 minutes or until the bacon becomes browned and crispy. 4. Make the sauce: Stir all the ingredients for the sauce in a small bowl. Wrap the bowl in plastic and set in the refrigerator until ready to serve. 5. Transfer the hot dogs to a platter and serve hot with the sauce.

Mustard Herb Pork Tenderloin

Prep time: 5 minutes | Cook time: 20 minutes | Serves 6

60 ml mayonnaise	1 (450 g) pork tenderloin
2 tablespoons Dijon mustard	½ teaspoon salt
½ teaspoon dried thyme	¼ teaspoon ground black pepper
¼ teaspoon dried rosemary	

1. In a small bowl, mix mayonnaise, mustard, thyme, and rosemary. Brush tenderloin with mixture on all sides, then sprinkle with salt and pepper on all sides. 2. Place tenderloin into ungreased air fryer basket. Adjust the temperature to 204ºC and air fry for 20 minutes, turning tenderloin halfway through cooking. Tenderloin will be golden and have an internal temperature of at least 64ºC when done. Serve warm.

Italian Steak Rolls

Prep time: 30 minutes | Cook time: 9 minutes | Serves 4

1 tablespoon vegetable oil
2 cloves garlic, minced
2 teaspoons dried Italian seasoning
1 teaspoon coarse or flaky salt
1 teaspoon black pepper
450 g bavette or skirt steak, ¼ to ½ inch thick

1 (280 g) package frozen spinach, thawed and squeezed dry
120 ml diced jarred roasted red pepper
235 ml shredded Mozzarella cheese

1. In a large bowl, combine the oil, garlic, Italian seasoning, salt, and pepper. Whisk to combine. Add the steak to the bowl, turning to ensure the entire steak is covered with the seasonings. Cover and marinate at room temperature for 30 minutes or in the refrigerator for up to 24 hours. 2. Lay the steak on a flat surface. Spread the spinach evenly over the steak, leaving a ¼-inch border at the edge. Evenly top each steak with the red pepper and cheese. 3. Starting at a long end, roll up the steak as tightly as possible, ending seam side down. Use 2 or 3 wooden toothpicks to hold the roll together. Using a sharp knife, cut the roll in half so that it better fits in the air fryer basket. 4. Place the steak roll, seam side down, in the air fryer basket. Set the air fryer to 204°C for 9 minutes. Use a meat thermometer to ensure the steak has reached an internal temperature of 64°C. (It is critical to not overcook bavette steak, so as to not toughen the meat.) 5. Let the steak rest for 10 minutes before cutting into slices to serve.

Spicy Lamb Sirloin Chops

Prep time: 30 minutes | Cook time: 15 minutes | Serves 4

½ brown onion, coarsely chopped
4 coin-size slices peeled fresh ginger
5 garlic cloves
1 teaspoon garam masala
1 teaspoon ground fennel

1 teaspoon ground cinnamon
1 teaspoon ground turmeric
½ to 1 teaspoon cayenne pepper
½ teaspoon ground cardamom
1 teaspoon coarse or flaky salt
450 g lamb sirloin chops

1. In a blender, combine the onion, ginger, garlic, garam masala, fennel, cinnamon, turmeric, cayenne, cardamom, and salt. Pulse until the onion is finely minced and the mixture forms a thick paste, 3 to 4 minutes. 2. Place the lamb chops in a large bowl. Slash the meat and fat with a sharp knife several times to allow the marinade to penetrate better. Add the spice paste to the bowl and toss the lamb to coat. Marinate at room temperature for 30 minutes or cover and refrigerate for up to 24 hours. 3. Place the lamb chops in a single layer in the air fryer basket. Set the air fryer to 164°C for 15 minutes, turning the chops halfway through the cooking time. Use a meat thermometer to ensure the lamb has reached an internal temperature of 64°C (medium-rare).

Pork Kebab with Yogurt Sauce

Prep time: 25 minutes | Cook time: 12 minutes | Serves 4

2 teaspoons olive oil
230 g pork mince
230 g beef mince
1 egg, whisked
Sea salt and ground black pepper, to taste
1 teaspoon paprika
2 garlic cloves, minced
1 teaspoon dried marjoram
1 teaspoon mustard seeds

½ teaspoon celery salt
Yogurt Sauce:
2 tablespoons olive oil
2 tablespoons fresh lemon juice
Sea salt, to taste
¼ teaspoon red pepper flakes, crushed
120 ml full-fat yogurt
1 teaspoon dried dill

1. Spritz the sides and bottom of the air fryer basket with 2 teaspoons of olive oil. 2. In a mixing dish, thoroughly combine the pork, beef, egg, salt, black pepper, paprika, garlic, marjoram, mustard seeds, and celery salt. 3. Form the mixture into kebabs and transfer them to the greased basket. Cook at 185°C for 11 to 12 minutes, turning them over once or twice. In the meantime, mix all the sauce ingredients and place in the refrigerator until ready to serve. Serve the pork kebabs with the yogurt sauce on the side. Enjoy!

Lamb Chops with Horseradish Sauce

Prep time: 30 minutes | Cook time: 13 minutes | Serves 4

Lamb:
4 lamb loin chops
2 tablespoons vegetable oil
1 clove garlic, minced
½ teaspoon coarse or flaky salt
½ teaspoon black pepper
Horseradish Cream Sauce:

120 ml mayonnaise
1 tablespoon Dijon mustard
1 to 1½ tablespoons grated horseradish
2 teaspoons sugar
Vegetable oil spray

1. For the lamb: Brush the lamb chops with the oil, rub with the garlic, and sprinkle with the salt and pepper. Marinate at room temperature for 30 minutes. 2. Meanwhile, for the sauce: In a medium bowl, combine the mayonnaise, mustard, horseradish, and sugar. Stir until well combined. Set aside half of the sauce for serving. 3. Spray the air fryer basket with vegetable oil spray and place the chops in the basket. Set the air fryer to 164°C for 10 minutes, turning the chops halfway through the cooking time. 4. Remove the chops from the air fryer and add to the bowl with the horseradish sauce, turning to coat with the sauce. Place the chops back in the air fryer basket. Set the air fryer to 204°C for 3 minutes. Use a meat thermometer to ensure the meat has reached an internal temperature of 64°C (for medium-rare). 5. Serve the chops with the reserved horseradish sauce.

Beef Burgers with Mushroom

Prep time: 10 minutes | Cook time: 21 to 23 minutes | Serves 4

450 g beef mince, formed into 4 patties
Sea salt and freshly ground black pepper, to taste
235 ml thinly sliced onion

230 g mushrooms, sliced
1 tablespoon avocado oil
60 g Gruyère cheese, shredded (about 120 ml)

1. Season the patties on both sides with salt and pepper. 2. Set the air fryer to 192°C. Place the patties in the basket and cook for 3 minutes. Flip and cook for another 2 minutes. Remove the burgers and set aside. 3. Place the onion and mushrooms in a medium bowl. Add the avocado oil and salt and pepper to taste; toss well. 4. Place the onion and mushrooms in the air fryer basket. Cook for 15 minutes, stirring occasionally. 5. Spoon the onions and mushrooms over the patties. Top with the cheese. Place the patties back in the air fryer basket and cook for another 1 to 3 minutes, until the cheese melts and an instant-read thermometer reads 72°C. Remove and let rest. The temperature will rise to 74°C, yielding a perfect medium-well burger.

Lamb Burger with Feta and Olives

Prep time: 10 minutes | Cook time: 20 minutes | Serves 3 to 4

2 teaspoons olive oil
⅓ onion, finely chopped
1 clove garlic, minced
450 g lamb mince
2 tablespoons fresh parsley, finely chopped
1½ teaspoons fresh oregano, finely chopped

120 ml black olives, finely chopped
80 ml crumbled feta cheese
½ teaspoon salt
Freshly ground black pepper, to taste
4 thick pitta breads

1. Preheat a medium skillet over medium-high heat on the stovetop. Add the olive oil and cook the onion until tender, but not browned, about 4 to 5 minutes. Add the garlic and cook for another minute. Transfer the onion and garlic to a mixing bowl and add the lamb mince, parsley, oregano, olives, feta cheese, salt and pepper. Gently mix the ingredients together. 2. Divide the mixture into 3 or 4 equal portions and then form the hamburgers, being careful not to over-handle the meat. One good way to do this is to throw the meat back and forth between your hands like a baseball, packing the meat each time you catch it. Flatten the balls into patties, making an indentation in the center of each patty. Flatten the sides of the patties as well to make it easier to fit them into the air fryer basket. 3. Preheat the air fryer to 188°C. 4. If you don't have room for all four burgers, air fry two or three burgers at a time for 8 minutes at 188°C. Flip the burgers over and air fry for another 8 minutes.

If you cooked your burgers in batches, return the first batch of burgers to the air fryer for the last two minutes of cooking to reheat. This should give you a medium-well burger. If you'd prefer a medium-rare burger, shorten the cooking time to about 13 minutes. Remove the burgers to a resting plate and let the burgers rest for a few minutes before dressing and serving. 5. While the burgers are resting, toast the pitta breads in the air fryer for 2 minutes. Tuck the burgers into the toasted pitta breads, or wrap the pittas around the burgers and serve with a tzatziki sauce or some mayonnaise.

Ham Hock Mac and Cheese

Prep time: 20 minutes | Cook time: 25 minutes | Serves 4

2 large eggs, beaten
475 ml cottage cheese, full-fat or low-fat
475 ml grated sharp Cheddar cheese, divided
235 ml sour cream
½ teaspoon salt

1 teaspoon freshly ground black pepper
475 ml uncooked elbow macaroni
2 ham hocks (about 310 g each), meat removed and diced
1 to 2 tablespoons oil

1. In a large bowl, stir together the eggs, cottage cheese, 235 ml of the Cheddar cheese, sour cream, salt, and pepper. 2. Stir in the macaroni and the diced meat. 3. Preheat the air fryer to 182°C. Spritz a baking pan with oil. 4. Pour the macaroni mixture into the prepared pan, making sure all noodles are covered with sauce. 5. Cook for 12 minutes. Stir in the remaining 235 ml of Cheddar cheese, making sure all the noodles are covered with sauce. Cook for 13 minutes more, until the noodles are tender. Let rest for 5 minutes before serving.

Air Fryer Chicken-Fried Steak

Prep time: 5 minutes | Cook time: 20 minutes | Serves 4

450 g beef braising steak
700 ml low-fat milk, divided
1 teaspoon dried thyme
1 teaspoon dried rosemary

2 medium egg whites
235 ml gluten-free breadcrumbs
120 ml coconut flour
1 tablespoon Cajun seasoning

1. In a bowl, marinate the steak in 475 ml of milk for 30 to 45 minutes. 2. Remove the steak from milk, shake off the excess liquid, and season with the thyme and rosemary. Discard the milk. 3. In a shallow bowl, beat the egg whites with the remaining 235 ml of milk. 4. In a separate shallow bowl, combine the breadcrumbs, coconut flour, and seasoning. 5. Dip the steak in the egg white mixture then dredge in the breadcrumb mixture, coating well. 6. Place the steak in the basket of an air fryer. 7. Set the air fryer to 200°C, close, and cook for 10 minutes. 8. Open the air fryer, turn the steaks, close, and cook for 10 minutes. Let rest for 5 minutes.

Savory Sausage Cobbler

Prep time: 15 minutes | Cook time: 34 minutes | Serves 4

Filling:
450 g Italian-seasoned sausage meat, removed from casing
235 ml sliced mushrooms
1 teaspoon fine sea salt
475 ml marinara sauce
Biscuits:
3 large egg whites

180 ml blanched almond flour
1 teaspoon baking powder
¼ teaspoon fine sea salt
2½ tablespoons very cold unsalted butter, cut into ¼-inch pieces
Fresh basil leaves, for garnish

1. Preheat the air fryer to 204°C. 2. Place the sausage in a pie pan (or a pan that fits into your air fryer). Use your hands to break up the sausage and spread it evenly on the bottom of the pan. Place the pan in the air fryer and air fry for 5 minutes. 3. Remove the pan from the air fryer and use a fork or metal spatula to crumble the sausage more. Season the mushrooms with the salt and add them to the pie pan. Stir to combine the mushrooms and sausage, then return the pan to the air fryer and air fry for 4 minutes, or until the mushrooms are soft and the sausage is cooked through. 4. Remove the pan from the air fryer. Add the marinara sauce and stir well. Set aside. 5. Make the biscuits: Place the egg whites in a large mixing bowl or the bowl of a stand mixer. Using a hand mixer or stand mixer, whip the egg whites until stiff peaks form. 6. In a medium-sized bowl, whisk together the almond flour, baking powder, and salt, then cut in the butter. Gently fold the flour mixture into the egg whites with a rubber spatula. 7. Using a large spoon or ice cream scoop, spoon one-quarter of the dough on top of the sausage mixture, making sure the butter stays in separate clumps. Repeat with the remaining dough, spacing the biscuits about 1 inch apart. 8. Place the pan in the air fryer and cook for 5 minutes, then lower the heat to 164°C and bake for another 15 to 20 minutes, until the biscuits are golden brown. Serve garnished with fresh basil leaves. 9. Store leftovers in an airtight container in the refrigerator for up to 3 days. Reheat in a preheated 176°C air fryer for 5 minutes, or until warmed through.

Spinach and Mozzarella Steak Rolls

Prep time: 10 minutes | Cook time: 12 minutes |
Makes 8 rolls

1 (450 g) bavette or skirt steak, butterflied
8 (30 g, ¼-inch-thick) slices low-moisture Mozzarella or other melting cheese

235 ml fresh spinach leaves
½ teaspoon salt
¼ teaspoon ground black pepper

1. Place steak on a large plate. Place Mozzarella slices to cover steak, leaving 1-inch at the edges. Lay spinach leaves over cheese. Gently roll steak and tie with kitchen twine or secure with toothpicks. Carefully slice into eight pieces. Sprinkle each with salt and pepper. 2. Place rolls into ungreased air fryer basket, cut side up. Adjust the temperature to 204°C and air fry for 12 minutes. Steak rolls will be browned and cheese will be melted when done and have an internal temperature of at least 64°C for medium steak and 82°C for well-done steak. Serve warm.

Buttery Pork Chops

Prep time: 5 minutes | Cook time: 12 minutes | Serves 4

4 (110 g) boneless pork chops
½ teaspoon salt
¼ teaspoon ground black

pepper
2 tablespoons salted butter, softened

1. Sprinkle pork chops on all sides with salt and pepper. Place chops into ungreased air fryer basket in a single layer. Adjust the temperature to 204°C and air fry for 12 minutes. Pork chops will be golden and have an internal temperature of at least 64°C when done. 2. Use tongs to remove cooked pork chops from air fryer and place onto a large plate. Top each chop with ½ tablespoon butter and let sit 2 minutes to melt. Serve warm.

Rack of Lamb with Pistachio Crust

Prep time: 10 minutes | Cook time: 19 minutes | Serves 2

120 ml finely chopped pistachios
3 tablespoons panko bread crumbs
1 teaspoon chopped fresh rosemary
2 teaspoons chopped fresh

oregano
Salt and freshly ground black pepper, to taste
1 tablespoon olive oil
1 rack of lamb, bones trimmed of fat and frenched
1 tablespoon Dijon mustard

1. Preheat the air fryer to 192°C. 2. Combine the pistachios, bread crumbs, rosemary, oregano, salt and pepper in a small bowl. (This is a good job for your food processor if you have one.) Drizzle in the olive oil and stir to combine. 3. Season the rack of lamb with salt and pepper on all sides and transfer it to the air fryer basket with the fat side facing up. Air fry the lamb for 12 minutes. Remove the lamb from the air fryer and brush the fat side of the lamb rack with the Dijon mustard. Coat the rack with the pistachio mixture, pressing the bread crumbs onto the lamb with your hands and rolling the bottom of the rack in any of the crumbs that fall off. 4. Return the rack of lamb to the air fryer and air fry for another 3 to 7 minutes or until an instant read thermometer reads 60°C for medium. Add or subtract a couple of minutes for lamb that is more or less well cooked. (Your time will vary depending on how big the rack of lamb is.) 5. Let the lamb rest for at least 5 minutes. Then, slice into chops and serve.

Italian Lamb Chops with Avocado Mayo

Prep time: 5 minutes | Cook time: 12 minutes | Serves 2

2 lamp chops
2 teaspoons Italian herbs
2 avocados

120 ml mayonnaise
1 tablespoon lemon juice

1. Season the lamb chops with the Italian herbs, then set aside for 5 minutes. 2. Preheat the air fryer to 204ºC and place the rack inside. 3. Put the chops on the rack and air fry for 12 minutes. 4. In the meantime, halve the avocados and open to remove the pits. Spoon the flesh into a blender. 5. Add the mayonnaise and lemon juice and pulse until a smooth consistency is achieved. 6. Take care when removing the chops from the air fryer, then plate up and serve with the avocado mayo.

Beef Whirls

Prep time: 30 minutes | Cook time: 18 minutes | Serves 6

3 minute steaks (170 g each)
1 (450 g) bottle Italian dressing
235 ml Italian-style bread crumbs (or plain bread crumbs with
Italian seasoning to taste)
120 ml grated Parmesan cheese

1 teaspoon dried basil
1 teaspoon dried oregano
1 teaspoon dried parsley
60 ml beef stock
1 to 2 tablespoons oil

1. In a large resealable bag, combine the steaks and Italian dressing. Seal the bag and refrigerate to marinate for 2 hours. 2. In a medium bowl, whisk the bread crumbs, cheese, basil, oregano, and parsley until blended. Stir in the beef stock. 3. Place the steaks on a cutting board and cut each in half so you have 6 equal pieces. Sprinkle with the bread crumb mixture. Roll up the steaks, jelly roll-style, and secure with toothpicks. 4. Preheat the air fryer to 204ºC. 5. Place 3 roll-ups in the air fryer basket. 6. Cook for 5 minutes. Flip the roll-ups and spritz with oil. Cook for 4 minutes more until the internal temperature reaches 64ºC. Repeat with the remaining roll-ups. Let rest for 5 to 10 minutes before serving.

Chapter 4 Fish and Seafood

Cilantro Lime Baked Salmon

Prep time: 10 minutes | Cook time: 12 minutes | Serves 2

2 salmon fillets, 85 g each, skin removed

1 tablespoon salted butter, melted

1 teaspoon chilli powder

½ teaspoon finely minced garlic

20 g sliced pickled jalapeños

½ medium lime, juiced

2 tablespoons chopped coriander

1. Place salmon fillets into a round baking pan. Brush each with butter and sprinkle with chilli powder and garlic. 2. Place jalapeño slices on top and around salmon. Pour half of the lime juice over the salmon and cover with foil. Place pan into the air fryer basket. 3. Adjust the temperature to 188°C and bake for 12 minutes. 4. When fully cooked, salmon should flake easily with a fork and reach an internal temperature of at least 64°C. 5. To serve, spritz with remaining lime juice and garnish with coriander.

Sea Bass with Potato Scales

Prep time: 10 minutes | Cook time: 10 minutes | Serves 2

2 fillets of sea bass, 170- to 230 g each

Salt and freshly ground black pepper, to taste

60 ml mayonnaise

2 teaspoons finely chopped lemon zest

1 teaspoon chopped fresh thyme

2 Fingerling, or new potatoes,

very thinly sliced into rounds

Olive oil

½ clove garlic, crushed into a paste

1 tablespoon capers, drained and rinsed

1 tablespoon olive oil

1 teaspoon lemon juice, to taste

1. Preheat the air fryer to 204°C. 2. Season the fish well with salt and freshly ground black pepper. Mix the mayonnaise, lemon zest and thyme together in a small bowl. Spread a thin layer of the mayonnaise mixture on both fillets. Start layering rows of potato slices onto the fish fillets to simulate the fish scales. The second row should overlap the first row slightly. Dabbing a little more mayonnaise along the upper edge of the row of potatoes where the next row overlaps will help the potato slices stick. Press the potatoes onto the fish to secure them well and season again with salt. Brush or spray the potato layer with olive oil. 3. Transfer the fish to the air fryer and air fry for 8 to 10 minutes, depending on the thickness of your fillets. 1-inch of fish should take 10 minutes at 204°C. 4. While the fish is cooking, add the garlic, capers, olive oil

and lemon juice to the remaining mayonnaise mixture to make the caper aïoli. 5. Serve the fish warm with a dollop of the aïoli on top or on the side.

BBQ Prawns with Creole Butter Sauce

Prep time: 10 minutes | Cook time: 12 to 15 minutes | Serves 4

6 tablespoons unsalted butter

80 ml Worcestershire sauce

3 cloves garlic, minced

Juice of 1 lemon

1 teaspoon paprika

1 teaspoon Creole seasoning

680 g large uncooked prawns, peeled and deveined

2 tablespoons fresh parsley

1. Preheat the air fryer to 188°C. 2. In a large microwave-safe bowl, combine the butter, Worcestershire, and garlic. Microwave on high for 1 to 2 minutes until the butter is melted. Stir in the lemon juice, paprika, and Creole seasoning. Add the prawns and toss until thoroughly coated. 3. Transfer the mixture to a casserole dish or pan that fits in your air fryer. Pausing halfway through the cooking time to turn the prawns, air fry for 12 to 15 minutes, until the prawns are cooked through. Top with the parsley just before serving.

Salmon Spring Rolls

Prep time: 20 minutes | Cook time: 8 to 10 minutes | Serves 4

230 g salmon fillet

1 teaspoon toasted sesame oil

1 onion, sliced

8 rice paper wrappers

1 yellow bell pepper, thinly

sliced

1 carrot, shredded

10 g chopped fresh flat-leaf parsley

15 g chopped fresh basil

1. Put the salmon in the air fryer basket and drizzle with the sesame oil. Add the onion. Air fry at 188°C for 8 to 10 minutes, or until the salmon just flakes when tested with a fork and the onion is tender. 2. Meanwhile, fill a small shallow bowl with warm water. One at a time, dip the rice paper wrappers into the water and place on a work surface. 3. Top each wrapper with one-eighth each of the salmon and onion mixture, yellow bell pepper, carrot, parsley, and basil. Roll up the wrapper, folding in the sides, to enclose the ingredients. 4. If you like, bake in the air fryer at 192°C for 7 to 9 minutes, until the rolls are crunchy. Cut the rolls in half to serve.

Crab and Bell Pepper Cakes

Prep time: 5 minutes | Cook time: 10 minutes | Serves 4

230 g jumbo lump crabmeat	1 egg
1 tablespoon Old Bay seasoning	60 g mayonnaise
40 g bread crumbs	Juice of ½ lemon
40 g diced red bell pepper	1 teaspoon plain flour
40 g diced green bell pepper	Cooking oil spray

1. Sort through the crabmeat, picking out any bits of shell or cartilage. 2. In a large bowl, stir together the Old Bay seasoning, bread crumbs, red and green bell peppers, egg, mayonnaise, and lemon juice. Gently stir in the crabmeat. 3. Insert the crisper plate into the basket and the basket into the unit. Preheat the unit to 192°C. 4. Form the mixture into 4 patties. Sprinkle ¼ teaspoon of flour on top of each patty. 5. Once the unit is preheated, spray the crisper plate with cooking oil. Place the crab cakes into the basket and spray them with cooking oil. 6. Cook for 10 minutes. 7. When the cooking is complete, the crab cakes will be golden brown and firm.

Tuna Avocado Bites

Prep time: 10 minutes | Cook time: 7 minutes | Makes 12 bites

280 g can tuna, drained	pitted, and mashed
60 ml full-fat mayonnaise	50 g blanched finely ground
1 stalk celery, chopped	almond flour, divided
1 medium avocado, peeled,	2 teaspoons coconut oil

1. In a large bowl, mix tuna, mayonnaise, celery, and mashed avocado. Form the mixture into balls. 2. Roll balls in almond flour and spritz with coconut oil. Place balls into the air fryer basket. 3. Adjust the temperature to 204°C and set the timer for 7 minutes. 4. Gently turn tuna bites after 5 minutes. Serve warm.

chilli Prawns

Prep time: 10 minutes | Cook time: 8 minutes | Serves 2

8 prawns, peeled and deveined	½ teaspoon garlic powder
Salt and black pepper, to taste	½ teaspoon ground cumin
½ teaspoon ground cayenne	½ teaspoon red chilli flakes
pepper	Cooking spray

1. Preheat the air fryer to 172°C. Spritz the air fryer basket with cooking spray. 2. Toss the remaining ingredients in a large bowl until the prawns are well coated. 3. Spread the coated prawns evenly in the basket and spray them with cooking spray. 4. Air fry for 8 minutes, flipping the prawns halfway through, or until the prawns are pink. 5. Remove the prawns from the basket to a plate.

Marinated Salmon Fillets

Prep time: 10 minutes | Cook time: 15 to 20 minutes | Serves 4

60 ml soy sauce	½ teaspoon freshly ground
60 ml rice wine vinegar	black pepper
1 tablespoon brown sugar	½ teaspoon minced garlic
1 tablespoon olive oil	4 salmon fillets, 170 g each,
1 teaspoon mustard powder	skin-on
1 teaspoon ground ginger	Cooking spray

1. In a small bowl, combine the soy sauce, rice wine vinegar, brown sugar, olive oil, mustard powder, ginger, black pepper, and garlic to make a marinade. 2. Place the fillets in a shallow baking dish and pour the marinade over them. Cover the baking dish and marinate for at least 1 hour in the refrigerator, turning the fillets occasionally to keep them coated in the marinade. 3. Preheat the air fryer to 188°C. Spray the air fryer basket lightly with cooking spray. 4. Shake off as much marinade as possible from the fillets and place them, skin-side down, in the air fryer basket in a single layer. You may need to cook the fillets in batches. 5. Air fry for 15 to 20 minutes for well done. The minimum internal temperature should be 64°C at the thickest part of the fillets. 6. Serve hot.

Tuna Steak

Prep time: 10 minutes | Cook time: 12 minutes | Serves 4

455 g tuna steaks, boneless and	1 tablespoon avocado oil
cubed	1 tablespoon apple cider
1 tablespoon mustard	vinegar

1. Mix avocado oil with mustard and apple cider vinegar. 2. Then brush tuna steaks with mustard mixture and put in the air fryer basket. 3. Cook the fish at 182°C for 6 minutes per side.

Air Fryer Fish Fry

Prep time: 5 minutes | Cook time: 15 minutes | Serves 4

470 ml low-fat buttermilk	70 g plain yellow cornmeal
½ teaspoon garlic powder	45 g chickpea flour
½ teaspoon onion powder	¼ teaspoon cayenne pepper
4 (110 g) sole fillets	Freshly ground black pepper

1. In a large bowl, combine the buttermilk, garlic powder, and onion powder. 2. Add the sole, turning until well coated, and set aside to marinate for 20 minutes. 3. In a shallow bowl, stir the cornmeal, chickpea flour, cayenne, and pepper together. 4. Dredge the fillets in the meal mixture, turning until well coated. Place in the basket of an air fryer. 5. Set the air fryer to 192°C, close, and cook for 12 minutes.

Crab Cakes with Lettuce and Apple Salad

Prep time: 10 minutes | Cook time: 13 minutes | Serves 2

230 g lump crab meat, picked over for shells
2 tablespoons panko bread crumbs
1 spring onions, minced
1 large egg
1 tablespoon mayonnaise
1½ teaspoons Dijon mustard
Pinch of cayenne pepper
2 shallots, sliced thin
1 tablespoon extra-virgin olive oil, divided
1 teaspoon lemon juice, plus lemon wedges for serving
⅛ teaspoon salt
Pinch of pepper
85 g small head round lettuce, torn into bite-size pieces
½ apple, cored and sliced thin

1. Preheat the air fryer to 204ºC. 2. Line large plate with triple layer of paper towels. Transfer crab meat to prepared plate and pat dry with additional paper towels. Combine panko, spring onion, egg, mayonnaise, mustard, and cayenne in a bowl. Using a rubber spatula, gently fold in crab meat until combined; discard paper towels. Divide crab mixture into 4 tightly packed balls, then flatten each into 1-inch-thick cake (cakes will be delicate). Transfer cakes to plate and refrigerate until firm, about 10 minutes. 3. Toss shallots with ½ teaspoon oil in separate bowl; transfer to air fryer basket. Air fry until shallots are browned, 5 to 7 minutes, tossing once halfway through cooking. Return shallots to now-empty bowl and set aside. 4. Arrange crab cakes in air fryer basket, spaced evenly apart. Return basket to air fryer and air fry until crab cakes are light golden brown on both sides, 8 to 10 minutes, flipping and rotating cakes halfway through cooking. 5. Meanwhile, whisk remaining 2½ teaspoons oil, lemon juice, salt, and pepper together in large bowl. Add lettuce, apple, and shallots and toss to coat. Serve crab cakes with salad, passing lemon wedges separately.

Almond-Crusted Fish

Prep time: 15 minutes | Cook time: 10 minutes | Serves 4

4 firm white fish fillets, 110g each
45 g breadcrumbs
20 g slivered almonds, crushed
2 tablespoons lemon juice
⅛ teaspoon cayenne
Salt and pepper, to taste
940 g plain flour
1 egg, beaten with 1 tablespoon water
Olive or vegetable oil for misting or cooking spray

1. Split fish fillets lengthwise down the center to create 8 pieces. 2. Mix breadcrumbs and almonds together and set aside. 3. Mix the lemon juice and cayenne together. Brush on all sides of fish. 4. Season fish to taste with salt and pepper. 5. Place the flour on a sheet of wax paper. 6. Roll fillets in flour, dip in egg wash, and roll in the crumb mixture. 7. Mist both sides of fish with oil or cooking spray. 8. Spray the air fryer basket and lay fillets inside. 9. Roast at 200ºC for 5 minutes, turn fish over, and cook for an additional 5 minutes or until fish is done and flakes easily.

Garlic Prawns

Prep time: 15 minutes | Cook time: 10 minutes | Serves 3

Prawns:
Olive or vegetable oil, for spraying
450 g medium raw prawns, peeled and deveined
6 tablespoons unsalted butter, melted
120 g panko bread crumbs
2 tablespoons garlic granules
1 teaspoon salt
½ teaspoon freshly ground black pepper
Garlic Butter Sauce:
115 g unsalted butter
2 teaspoons garlic granules
¾ teaspoon salt (omit if using salted butter)

Make the Prawns 1. Preheat the air fryer to 204ºC. Line the air fryer basket with baking paper and spray lightly with oil. 2. Place the prawns and melted butter in a zip-top plastic bag, seal, and shake well, until evenly coated. 3. In a medium bowl, mix together the breadcrumbs, garlic, salt, and black pepper. 4. Add the prawns to the panko mixture and toss until evenly coated. Shake off any excess coating. 5. Place the prawns in the prepared basket and spray lightly with oil. 6. Cook for 8 to 10 minutes, flipping and spraying with oil after 4 to 5 minutes, until golden brown and crispy. Make the Garlic Butter Sauce 7. In a microwave-safe bowl, combine the butter, garlic, and salt and microwave on 50% power for 30 to 60 seconds, stirring every 15 seconds, until completely melted. 8. Serve the prawns immediately with the garlic butter sauce on the side for dipping.

Tuna Patties with Spicy Sriracha Sauce

Prep time: 10 minutes | Cook time: 10 minutes | Serves 4

2 (170 g) cans tuna packed in oil, drained
3 tablespoons almond flour
2 tablespoons mayonnaise
1 teaspoon dried dill
½ teaspoon onion powder
Pinch of salt and pepper
Spicy Sriracha Sauce:
60 g mayonnaise
1 tablespoon Sriracha sauce
1 teaspoon garlic powder

1. Preheat the air fryer to 192ºC. Line the basket with baking paper. 2. In a large bowl, combine the tuna, almond flour, mayonnaise, dill, and onion powder. Season to taste with salt and freshly ground black pepper. Use a fork to stir, mashing with the back of the fork as necessary, until thoroughly combined. 3. Use an ice cream scoop to form the tuna mixture patties. Place the patties in a single layer on the baking paper in the air fryer basket. Press lightly with the bottom of the scoop to flatten into a circle about ½ inch thick. Pausing halfway through the cooking time to turn the patties, air fry for 10 minutes until lightly browned. 4. To make the Sriracha sauce: In a small bowl, combine the mayonnaise, Sriracha, and garlic powder. Serve the tuna patties topped with the Sriracha sauce.

Bacon-Wrapped Scallops

Prep time: 5 minutes | Cook time: 10 minutes | Serves 4

8 sea scallops, 30 g each, cleaned and patted dry
8 slices bacon
¼ teaspoon salt
¼ teaspoon ground black pepper

1. Wrap each scallop in 1 slice bacon and secure with a toothpick. Sprinkle with salt and pepper. 2. Place scallops into ungreased air fryer basket. Adjust the temperature to 182ºC and air fry for 10 minutes. Scallops will be opaque and firm, and have an internal temperature of 56ºC when done. Serve warm.

Creamy Haddock

Prep time: 10 minutes | Cook time: 8 minutes | Serves 4

455 g haddock fillet
1 teaspoon cayenne pepper
1 teaspoon salt
1 teaspoon coconut oil
120 ml heavy cream

1. Grease a baking pan with coconut oil. 2. Then put haddock fillet inside and sprinkle it with cayenne pepper, salt, and heavy cream. Put the baking pan in the air fryer basket and cook at 192ºC for 8 minutes.

Chilli Tilapia

Prep time: 5 minutes | Cook time: 20 minutes | Serves 4

4 tilapia fillets, boneless
1 teaspoon chilli flakes
1 teaspoon dried oregano
1 tablespoon avocado oil
1 teaspoon mustard

1. Rub the tilapia fillets with chilli flakes, dried oregano, avocado oil, and mustard and put in the air fryer. 2. Cook it for 10 minutes per side at 182ºC.

Crab Legs

Prep time: 5 minutes | Cook time: 15 minutes | Serves 4

60 g salted butter, melted and divided
1.4 kg crab legs
¼ teaspoon garlic powder
Juice of ½ medium lemon

1. In a large bowl, drizzle 2 tablespoons butter over crab legs. Place crab legs into the air fryer basket. 2. Adjust the temperature to 204ºC and air fry for 15 minutes. 3. Shake the air fryer basket to toss the crab legs halfway through the cooking time. 4. In a small bowl, mix remaining butter, garlic powder, and lemon juice. 5. To serve, crack open crab legs and remove meat. Dip in lemon butter.

Maple Balsamic Glazed Salmon

Prep time: 5 minutes | Cook time: 10 minutes | Serves 4

4 fillets of salmon, 170 g each
Salt and freshly ground black pepper, to taste
Vegetable oil
60 ml pure maple syrup
3 tablespoons balsamic vinegar
1 teaspoon Dijon mustard

1. Preheat the air fryer to 204ºC. 2. Season the salmon well with salt and freshly ground black pepper. Spray or brush the bottom of the air fryer basket with vegetable oil and place the salmon fillets inside. Air fry the salmon for 5 minutes. 3. While the salmon is air frying, combine the maple syrup, balsamic vinegar and Dijon mustard in a small saucepan over medium heat and stir to blend well. Let the mixture simmer while the fish is cooking. It should start to thicken slightly, but keep your eye on it so it doesn't burn. 4. Brush the glaze on the salmon fillets and air fry for an additional 5 minutes. The salmon should feel firm to the touch when finished and the glaze should be nicely browned on top. Brush a little more glaze on top before removing and serving with rice and vegetables, or a nice green salad.

Mackerel with Spinach

Prep time: 15 minutes | Cook time: 20 minutes | Serves 5

455 g mackerel, trimmed
1 bell pepper, chopped
15 g spinach, chopped
1 tablespoon avocado oil
1 teaspoon ground black pepper
1 teaspoon tomato paste

1. In the mixing bowl, mix bell pepper with spinach, ground black pepper, and tomato paste. 2. Fill the mackerel with spinach mixture. 3. Then brush the fish with avocado oil and put it in the air fryer. 4. Cook the fish at 185ºC for 20 minutes.

Fish Taco Bowl

Prep time: 10 minutes | Cook time: 12 minutes | Serves 4

½ teaspoon salt
¼ teaspoon garlic powder
¼ teaspoon ground cumin
4 cod fillets, 110 g each
360 g finely shredded green
cabbage
735 g mayonnaise
¼ teaspoon ground black pepper
20 g chopped pickled jalapeños

1. Sprinkle salt, garlic powder, and cumin over cod and place into ungreased air fryer basket. Adjust the temperature to 176ºC and air fry for 12 minutes, turning fillets halfway through cooking. Cod will flake easily and have an internal temperature of at least 64ºC when done. 2. In a large bowl, toss cabbage with mayonnaise, pepper, and jalapeños until fully coated. Serve cod warm over cabbage slaw on four medium plates.

Chinese Ginger-Spring Onion Fish

Prep time: 15 minutes | Cook time: 15 minutes | Serves 2

Bean Sauce:
2 tablespoons soy sauce
1 tablespoon rice wine
1 tablespoon doubanjiang
(Chinese black bean paste)
1 teaspoon minced fresh ginger
1 clove garlic, minced
Vegetables and Fish:
1 tablespoon peanut oil
235 g julienned spring onions
(white and green parts)
5 g chopped fresh coriander
2 tablespoons julienned fresh
ginger
2 (170) g white fish fillets, such
as tilapia

Bean Sauce:
2 tablespoons soy sauce
1 tablespoon rice wine
1 tablespoon doubanjiang
(Chinese black bean paste)
1 teaspoon minced fresh ginger
1 clove garlic, minced
Vegetables and Fish:
1 tablespoon peanut oil
235 g julienned spring onions
(white and green parts)
5 g chopped fresh coriander
2 tablespoons julienned fresh
ginger
2 (170 g) white fish fillets, such
as tilapia

1. For the sauce: In a small bowl, combine all the ingredients and stir until well combined; set aside. 2. For the vegetables and fish: In a medium bowl, combine the peanut oil, spring onions, coriander, and ginger. Toss to combine. 3. Cut two squares of baking paper large enough to hold one fillet and half of the vegetables. Place one fillet on each baking paper square, top with the vegetables, and pour over the sauce. Fold over the baking paper and crimp the sides in small, tight folds to hold the fish, vegetables, and sauce securely inside the packet. 4. Place the packets in a single layer in the air fryer basket. Set fryer to 176°C for 15 minutes. 5. Transfer each packet to a dinner plate. Cut open with scissors just before serving. 1. For the sauce: In a small bowl, combine all the ingredients and stir until well combined; set aside. 2. For the vegetables and fish: In a medium bowl, combine the peanut oil, spring onions, coriander, and ginger. Toss to combine. 3. Cut two squares of baking paper large enough to hold one fillet and half of the vegetables. Place one fillet on each baking paper square, top with the vegetables, and pour over the sauce. Fold over the parchment paper and crimp the sides in small, tight folds to hold the fish, vegetables, and sauce securely inside the packet. 4. Place the packets in a single layer in the air fryer basket. Cook for 15 minutes. 5. Transfer each packet to a dinner plate. Cut open with scissors just before serving. 1. For the sauce: In a small bowl, combine all the ingredients and stir until well combined; set aside. 2. For the vegetables and fish: In a medium bowl, combine the peanut oil, spring onions, coriander, and ginger. Toss to combine. 3. Cut two squares of baking paper large enough to hold one fillet and half of the vegetables. Place one fillet on each baking paper square, top with the vegetables, and pour over the sauce. Fold over the baking paper and crimp the sides in small, tight folds to hold the fish, vegetables, and sauce securely inside the packet. 4. Place the packets in a single layer in the air fryer basket. Keep fryer at 176°C and cook for 15 minutes. 5. Transfer each packet to a dinner plate. Cut open with scissors just before serving.

Roasted Halibut Steaks with Parsley

Prep time: 5 minutes | Cook time: 10 minutes | Serves 4

455 g halibut steaks
60 ml vegetable oil
2½ tablespoons Worcester
sauce
2 tablespoons honey
2 tablespoons vermouth or
white wine vinegar

1 tablespoon freshly squeezed
lemon juice
1 tablespoon fresh parsley
leaves, coarsely chopped
Salt and pepper, to taste
1 teaspoon dried basil

1. Preheat the air fryer to 200°C. 2. Put all the ingredients in a large mixing dish and gently stir until the fish is coated evenly. 3. Transfer the fish to the air fryer basket and roast for 10 minutes, flipping the fish halfway through, or until the fish reaches an internal temperature of at least 64°C on a meat thermometer. 4. Let the fish cool for 5 minutes and serve.

Fish Gratin

Prep time: 30 minutes | Cook time: 17 minutes | Serves 4

1 tablespoon avocado oil
455 g hake fillets
1 teaspoon garlic powder
Sea salt and ground white
pepper, to taste
2 tablespoons shallots, chopped
1 bell pepper, seeded and

chopped
110 g cottage cheese
120 ml sour cream
1 egg, well whisked
1 teaspoon yellow mustard
1 tablespoon lime juice
60 g Swiss cheese, shredded

1. Brush the bottom and sides of a casserole dish with avocado oil. Add the hake fillets to the casserole dish and sprinkle with garlic powder, salt, and pepper. 2. Add the chopped shallots and bell peppers. 3. In a mixing bowl, thoroughly combine the Cottage cheese, sour cream, egg, mustard, and lime juice. Pour the mixture over fish and spread evenly. 4. Cook in the preheated air fryer at 188°C for 10 minutes. 5. Top with the Swiss cheese and cook an additional 7 minutes. Let it rest for 10 minutes before slicing and serving. Bon appétit!

Tuna Cakes

Prep time: 10 minutes | Cook time: 10 minutes | Serves 4

4 (85 g) tuna fillets, drained
1 large egg, whisked
2 tablespoons peeled and

chopped white onion
½ teaspoon Old Bay seasoning

1. In a large bowl, mix all ingredients together and form into four patties. 2. Place patties into ungreased air fryer basket. Adjust the temperature to 204°C and air fry for 10 minutes. Patties will be browned and crispy when done. Let cool 5 minutes before serving.

Classic Fish Sticks with Tartar Sauce

Prep time: 10 minutes | Cook time: 12 to 15 minutes | Serves 4

680 g cod fillets, cut into 1-inch strips	120 ml sour cream
1 teaspoon salt	120 ml mayonnaise
½ teaspoon freshly ground black pepper	3 tablespoons chopped dill pickle
2 eggs	2 tablespoons capers, drained and chopped
70 g almond flour	½ teaspoon dried dill
20 g grated Parmesan cheese	1 tablespoon dill pickle liquid (optional)
Tartar Sauce:	

1. Preheat the air fryer to 204°C. 2. Season the cod with the salt and black pepper; set aside. 3. In a shallow bowl, lightly beat the eggs. In a second shallow bowl, combine the almond flour and Parmesan cheese. Stir until thoroughly combined. 4. Working with a few pieces at a time, dip the fish into the egg mixture followed by the flour mixture. Press lightly to ensure an even coating. 5. Working in batches if necessary, arrange the fish in a single layer in the air fryer basket and spray lightly with olive oil. Pausing halfway through the cooking time to turn the fish, air fry for 12 to 15 minutes, until the fish flakes easily with a fork. Let sit in the basket for a few minutes before serving with the tartar sauce. 6. To make the tartar sauce: In a small bowl, combine the sour cream, mayonnaise, pickle, capers, and dill. If you prefer a thinner sauce, stir in the pickle liquid.

Salmon Burgers with Creamy Broccoli Slaw

Prep time: 15 minutes | Cook time: 10 minutes | Serves 4

For the salmon burgers	For the broccoli slaw
455 g salmon fillets, bones and skin removed	270 g chopped or shredded broccoli
1 egg	25 g shredded carrots
10 g fresh dill, chopped	30 g sunflower seeds
60 g fresh whole wheat bread crumbs	2 garlic cloves, minced
½ teaspoon salt	½ teaspoon salt
½ teaspoon cayenne pepper	2 tablespoons apple cider vinegar
2 garlic cloves, minced	285 g nonfat plain Greek yogurt
4 whole wheat buns	

Make the salmon burgers 1. Preheat the air fryer to 182°C. 2. In a food processor, pulse the salmon fillets until they are finely chopped. 3. In a large bowl, combine the chopped salmon, egg, dill, bread crumbs, salt, cayenne, and garlic until it comes together. 4. Form the salmon into 4 patties. Place them into the air fryer basket, making sure that they don't touch each other. 5. Bake for 5 minutes. Flip the salmon patties and bake for 5 minutes more. Make the broccoli slaw 6. In a large bowl, combine all of the ingredients for the broccoli slaw. Mix well. 7. Serve the salmon burgers on toasted whole wheat buns, and top with a generous portion of broccoli slaw.

Tuna with Herbs

Prep time: 20 minutes | Cook time: 17 minutes | Serves 4

1 tablespoon butter, melted	Sea salt and ground black pepper, to taste
1 medium-sized leek, thinly sliced	½ teaspoon dried rosemary
1 tablespoon chicken stock	½ teaspoon dried basil
1 tablespoon dry white wine	½ teaspoon dried thyme
455 g tuna	2 small ripe tomatoes, puréed
½ teaspoon red pepper flakes, crushed	120 g Parmesan cheese, grated

1. Melt ½ tablespoon of butter in a sauté pan over medium-high heat. Now, cook the leek and garlic until tender and aromatic. Add the stock and wine to deglaze the pan. 2. Preheat the air fryer to 188°C. 3. Grease a casserole dish with the remaining ½ tablespoon of melted butter. Place the fish in the casserole dish. Add the seasonings. Top with the sautéed leek mixture. Add the tomato purée. Cook for 10 minutes in the preheated air fryer. Top with grated Parmesan cheese; cook an additional 7 minutes until the crumbs are golden. Bon appétit!

Tuna Patty Sliders

Prep time: 15 minutes | Cook time: 10 to 15 minutes | Serves 4

3 cans tuna, 140 g each, packed in water	1 tablespoon Sriracha
40 g whole-wheat panko bread crumbs	¾ teaspoon black pepper
50 g shredded Parmesan cheese	10 whole-wheat buns
	Cooking spray

1. Preheat the air fryer to 176°C. 2. Spray the air fryer basket lightly with cooking spray. 3. In a medium bowl combine the tuna, bread crumbs, Parmesan cheese, Sriracha, and black pepper and stir to combine. 4. Form the mixture into 10 patties. 5. Place the patties in the air fryer basket in a single layer. Spray the patties lightly with cooking spray. You may need to cook them in batches. 6. Air fry for 6 to 8 minutes. Turn the patties over and lightly spray with cooking spray. Air fry until golden brown and crisp, another 4 to 7 more minutes. Serve warm.

Crispy Fish Sticks

Prep time: 15 minutes | Cook time: 10 minutes | Serves 4

30 g crushed panko breadcrumbs

25 g blanched finely ground almond flour

½ teaspoon Old Bay seasoning

1 tablespoon coconut oil

1 large egg

455 g cod fillet, cut into ¾-inch strips

1. Place panko, almond flour, Old Bay seasoning, and coconut oil into a large bowl and mix together. In a medium bowl, whisk egg. 2. Dip each fish stick into the egg and then gently press into the flour mixture, coating as fully and evenly as possible. Place fish sticks into the air fryer basket. 3. Adjust the temperature to 204ºC and air fry for 10 minutes or until golden. 4. Serve immediately.

Chapter 5 Poultry

Chicken Croquettes with Creole Sauce

Prep time: 30 minutes | Cook time: 10 minutes | Serves 4

280 g shredded cooked chicken
120 g shredded Cheddar cheese
2 eggs
15 g finely chopped onion
25 g almond meal
1 tablespoon poultry seasoning
Olive oil

Creole Sauce:
60 g mayonnaise
60 g sour cream
1½ teaspoons Dijon mustard
1½ teaspoons fresh lemon juice
½ teaspoon garlic powder
½ teaspoon Creole seasoning

1. In a large bowl, combine the chicken, Cheddar, eggs, onion, almond meal, and poultry seasoning. Stir gently until thoroughly combined. Cover and refrigerate for 30 minutes. 2. Meanwhile, to make the Creole sauce: In a small bowl, whisk together the mayonnaise, sour cream, Dijon mustard, lemon juice, garlic powder, and Creole seasoning until thoroughly combined. Cover and refrigerate until ready to serve. 3. Preheat the air fryer to 200°C. Divide the chicken mixture into 8 portions and shape into patties. 4. Working in batches if necessary, arrange the patties in a single layer in the air fryer basket and coat both sides lightly with olive oil. Pausing halfway through the cooking time to flip the patties, air fry for 10 minutes, or until lightly browned and the cheese is melted. Serve with the Creole sauce.

Jalapeño Popper Hasselback Chicken

Prep time: 10 minutes | Cook time: 19 minutes | Serves 2

Oil, for spraying
2 (230 g) boneless, skinless chicken breasts
60 g cream cheese, softened

55 g bacon bits
20 g chopped pickled jalapeños
40 g shredded Cheddar cheese, divided

1. Line the air fryer basket with parchment and spray lightly with oil. 2. Make multiple cuts across the top of each chicken breast, cutting only halfway through. 3. In a medium bowl, mix together the cream cheese, bacon bits, jalapeños, and Cheddar cheese. Spoon some of the mixture into each cut. 4. Place the chicken in the prepared basket. 5. Air fry at 176°C for 14 minutes. Scatter the remaining cheese on top of the chicken and cook for another 2 to 5 minutes, or until the cheese is melted and the internal temperature reaches 76°C.

Chicken Thighs with Coriander

Prep time: 15 minutes | Cook time: 25 minutes | Serves 4

1 tablespoon olive oil
Juice of ½ lime
1 tablespoon coconut aminos
1½ teaspoons Montreal chicken seasoning

8 bone-in chicken thighs, skin on
2 tablespoons chopped fresh coriander

1. In a gallon-size resealable bag, combine the olive oil, lime juice, coconut aminos, and chicken seasoning. Add the chicken thighs, seal the bag, and massage the bag to ensure the chicken is thoroughly coated. Refrigerate for at least 2 hours, preferably overnight. 2. Preheat the air fryer to 200°C. 3. Remove the chicken from the marinade (discard the marinade) and arrange in a single layer in the air fryer basket. Pausing halfway through the cooking time to flip the chicken, air fry for 20 to 25 minutes, until a thermometer inserted into the thickest part registers 76°C. 4. Transfer the chicken to a serving platter and top with the coriander before serving.

Buttermilk-Fried Drumsticks

Prep time: 10 minutes | Cook time: 25 minutes | Serves 2

1 egg
120 g buttermilk
90 g self-rising flour
90 g seasoned panko bread crumbs

1 teaspoon salt
¼ teaspoon ground black pepper (to mix into coating)
4 chicken drumsticks, skin on
Oil for misting or cooking spray

1. Beat together egg and buttermilk in shallow dish. 2. In a second shallow dish, combine the flour, panko crumbs, salt, and pepper. 3. Sprinkle chicken legs with additional salt and pepper to taste. 4. Dip legs in buttermilk mixture, then roll in panko mixture, pressing in crumbs to make coating stick. Mist with oil or cooking spray. 5. Spray the air fryer basket with cooking spray. 6. Cook drumsticks at 180°C for 10 minutes. Turn pieces over and cook an additional 10 minutes. 7. Turn pieces to check for browning. If you have any white spots that haven't begun to brown, spritz them with oil or cooking spray. Continue cooking for 5 more minutes or until crust is golden brown and juices run clear. Larger, meatier drumsticks will take longer to cook than small ones.

Spicy Chicken Thighs and Gold Potatoes

Prep time: 5 minutes | Cook time: 25 minutes | Serves 4

4 bone-in, skin-on chicken thighs

½ teaspoon kosher salt or ¼ teaspoon fine salt

2 tablespoons melted unsalted butter

2 teaspoons Worcestershire sauce

2 teaspoons curry powder

1 teaspoon dried oregano leaves

½ teaspoon dry mustard

½ teaspoon granulated garlic

¼ teaspoon paprika

¼ teaspoon hot pepper sauce

Cooking oil spray

4 medium Yukon gold potatoes, chopped

1 tablespoon extra-virgin olive oil

1. Sprinkle the chicken thighs on both sides with salt. 2. In a medium bowl, stir together the melted butter, Worcestershire sauce, curry powder, oregano, dry mustard, granulated garlic, paprika, and hot pepper sauce. Add the thighs to the sauce and stir to coat. 3. Insert the crisper plate into the basket and the basket into the unit. Preheat the unit by selecting AIR FRY, setting the temperature to 200ºC, and setting the time to 3 minutes. Select START/STOP to begin. 4. Once the unit is preheated, spray the crisper plate with cooking oil. In the basket, combine the potatoes and olive oil and toss to coat. 5. Add the wire rack to the air fryer and place the chicken thighs on top. 6. Select AIR FRY, set the temperature to 200ºC, and set the time to 25 minutes. Select START/STOP to begin. 7. After 19 minutes check the chicken thighs. If a food thermometer inserted into the chicken registers 76ºC, transfer them to a clean plate, and cover with aluminum foil to keep warm. If they aren't cooked to 76ºC, resume cooking for another 1 to 2 minutes until they are done. Remove them from the unit along with the rack. 8. Remove the basket and shake it to distribute the potatoes. Reinsert the basket to resume cooking for 3 to 6 minutes, or until the potatoes are crisp and golden brown. 9. When the cooking is complete, serve the chicken with the potatoes.

Chicken Wellington

Prep time: 30 minutes | Cook time: 31 minutes | Serves 2

2 (140 g) boneless, skinless chicken breasts

120 ml White Worcestershire sauce

3 tablespoons butter

25 g finely diced onion (about ½ onion)

225 g button mushrooms, finely chopped

60 ml chicken stock

2 tablespoons White Worcestershire sauce (or white wine)

Salt and freshly ground black pepper, to taste

1 tablespoon chopped fresh tarragon

2 sheets puff pastry, thawed

1 egg, beaten

Vegetable oil

1. Place the chicken breasts in a shallow dish. Pour the White Worcestershire sauce over the chicken coating both sides and marinate for 30 minutes. 2. While the chicken is marinating, melt the butter in a large skillet over medium-high heat on the stovetop. Add the onion and sauté for a few minutes, until it starts to soften. Add the mushrooms and sauté for 3 to 5 minutes until the vegetables are brown and soft. Deglaze the skillet with the chicken stock, scraping up any bits from the bottom of the pan. Add the White Worcestershire sauce and simmer for 2 to 3 minutes until the mixture reduces and starts to thicken. Season with salt and freshly ground black pepper. Remove the mushroom mixture from the heat and stir in the fresh tarragon. Let the mushroom mixture cool. 3. Preheat the air fryer to 180ºC. 4. Remove the chicken from the marinade and transfer it to the air fryer basket. Tuck the small end of the chicken breast under the thicker part to shape it into a circle rather than an oval. Pour the marinade over the chicken and air fry for 10 minutes. 5. Roll out the puff pastry and cut out two 6-inch squares. Brush the perimeter of each square with the egg wash. Place half of the mushroom mixture in the centre of each puff pastry square. Place the chicken breasts, top side down on the mushroom mixture. Starting with one corner of puff pastry and working in one direction, pull the pastry up over the chicken to enclose it and press the ends of the pastry together in the middle. Brush the pastry with the egg wash to seal the edges. Turn the Wellingtons over and set aside. 6. Make a decorative design with the remaining puff pastry, cut out four 10-inch strips. For each Wellington, twist two of the strips together, place them over the chicken breast wrapped in puff pastry, and tuck the ends underneath to seal it. Brush the entire top and sides of the Wellingtons with the egg wash. 7. Preheat the air fryer to 180ºC. . 8. Spray or brush the air fryer basket with vegetable oil. Air fry the chicken Wellingtons for 13 minutes. Carefully turn the Wellingtons over. Air fry for another 8 minutes. Transfer to serving plates, light a candle and enjoy!

Golden Chicken Cutlets

Prep time: 15 minutes | Cook time: 15 minutes | Serves 4

2 tablespoons panko breadcrumbs

20 g grated Parmesan cheese

⅛ tablespoon paprika

½ tablespoon garlic powder

2 large eggs

4 chicken cutlets

1 tablespoon parsley

Salt and ground black pepper, to taste

Cooking spray

1. Preheat air fryer to 200ºC. Spritz the air fryer basket with cooking spray. 2. Combine the breadcrumbs, Parmesan, paprika, garlic powder, salt, and ground black pepper in a large bowl. Stir to mix well. Beat the eggs in a separate bowl. 3. Dredge the chicken cutlets in the beaten eggs, then roll over the breadcrumbs mixture to coat well. Shake the excess off. 4. Transfer the chicken cutlets in the preheated air fryer and spritz with cooking spray. 5. Air fry for 15 minutes or until crispy and golden brown. Flip the cutlets halfway through. 6. Serve with parsley on top.

Chicken Pesto Pizzas

Prep time: 10 minutes | Cook time: 12 minutes | Serves 4

450 g chicken mince thighs	20 g basil pesto
¼ teaspoon salt	225 g shredded Mozzarella
⅛ teaspoon ground black	cheese
pepper	4 grape tomatoes, sliced

1. Cut four squares of parchment paper to fit into your air fryer basket. 2. Place chicken mince in a large bowl and mix with salt and pepper. Divide mixture into four equal sections. 3. Wet your hands with water to prevent sticking, then press each section into a 6-inch circle onto a piece of ungreased parchment. Place each chicken crust into air fryer basket, working in batches if needed. 4. Adjust the temperature to 180°C and air fry for 10 minutes, turning crusts halfway through cooking. 5. Spread 1 tablespoon pesto across the top of each crust, then sprinkle with ¼ of the Mozzarella and top with 1 sliced tomato. Continue cooking at 180°C for 2 minutes. Cheese will be melted and brown when done. Serve warm.

Spinach and Feta Stuffed Chicken Breasts

Prep time: 10 minutes | Cook time: 27 minutes | Serves 4

1 (280 g) package frozen	black pepper
spinach, thawed and drained	4 boneless chicken breasts
well	Salt and freshly ground black
80 g feta cheese, crumbled	pepper, to taste
½ teaspoon freshly ground	1 tablespoon olive oil

1. Prepare the filling. Squeeze out as much liquid as possible from the thawed spinach. Rough chop the spinach and transfer it to a mixing bowl with the feta cheese and the freshly ground black pepper. 2. Prepare the chicken breast. Place the chicken breast on a cutting board and press down on the chicken breast with one hand to keep it stabilized. Make an incision about 1-inch long in the fattest side of the breast. Move the knife up and down inside the chicken breast, without poking through either the top or the bottom, or the other side of the breast. The inside pocket should be about 3-inches long, but the opening should only be about 1-inch wide. If this is too difficult, you can make the incision longer, but you will have to be more careful when cooking the chicken breast since this will expose more of the stuffing. 3. Once you have prepared the chicken breasts, use your fingers to stuff the filling into each pocket, spreading the mixture down as far as you can. 4. Preheat the air fryer to 190°C. 5. Lightly brush or spray the air fryer basket and the chicken breasts with olive oil. Transfer two of the stuffed chicken breasts to the air fryer. Air fry for 12 minutes, turning the chicken breasts over halfway through the cooking time. Remove the chicken to a resting plate and air fry the second two breasts for 12 minutes. Return the first batch of chicken to the air fryer with the second batch and air fry for 3 more minutes. When the chicken is cooked, an instant read thermometer should register 76°C in the thickest part of the chicken, as well as in the stuffing. 6. Remove the chicken breasts and let them rest on a cutting board for 2 to 3 minutes. Slice the chicken on the bias and serve with the slices fanned out.

Curried Orange Honey Chicken

Prep time: 10 minutes | Cook time: 16 to 19 minutes | Serves 4

340 g boneless, skinless chicken	60 ml chicken stock
thighs, cut into 1-inch pieces	2 tablespoons honey
1 yellow bell pepper, cut into	60 ml orange juice
1½-inch pieces	1 tablespoon cornflour
1 small red onion, sliced	2 to 3 teaspoons curry powder
Olive oil for misting	

1. Preheat the air fryer to 190°C. 2. Put the chicken thighs, pepper, and red onion in the air fryer basket and mist with olive oil. 3. Roast for 12 to 14 minutes or until the chicken is cooked to 76°C, shaking the basket halfway through cooking time. 4. Remove the chicken and vegetables from the air fryer basket and set aside. 5. In a metal bowl, combine the stock, honey, orange juice, cornflour, and curry powder, and mix well. Add the chicken and vegetables, stir, and put the bowl in the basket. 6. Return the basket to the air fryer and roast for 2 minutes. Remove and stir, then roast for 2 to 3 minutes or until the sauce is thickened and bubbly. 7. Serve warm.

Pecan Turkey Cutlets

Prep time: 10 minutes | Cook time: 10 to 12 minutes per batch | Serves 4

90 g panko bread crumbs	30 g cornflour
¼ teaspoon salt	1 egg, beaten
¼ teaspoon pepper	450 g turkey cutlets, ½-inch
¼ teaspoon mustard powder	thick
¼ teaspoon poultry seasoning	Salt and pepper, to taste
50 g pecans	Oil for misting or cooking spray

1. Place the panko crumbs, ¼ teaspoon salt, ¼ teaspoon pepper, mustard, and poultry seasoning in food processor. Process until crumbs are finely crushed. Add pecans and process in short pulses just until nuts are finely chopped. Go easy so you don't overdo it! 2. Preheat the air fryer to 180°C. 3. Place cornflour in one shallow dish and beaten egg in another. Transfer coating mixture from food processor into a third shallow dish. 4. Sprinkle turkey cutlets with salt and pepper to taste. 5. Dip cutlets in cornflour and shake off excess. Then dip in beaten egg and roll in crumbs, pressing to coat well. Spray both sides with oil or cooking spray. 6. Place 2 cutlets in air fryer basket in a single layer and cook for 10 to 12 minutes or until juices run clear. 7. Repeat step 6 to cook remaining cutlets.

Buffalo Chicken Cheese Sticks

Prep time: 5 minutes | Cook time: 8 minutes | Serves 2

140 g shredded cooked chicken
60 ml buffalo sauce
220 g shredded Mozzarella

cheese
1 large egg
55 g crumbled feta

1. In a large bowl, mix all ingredients except the feta. Cut a piece of parchment to fit your air fryer basket and press the mixture into a ½-inch-thick circle. 2. Sprinkle the mixture with feta and place into the air fryer basket. 3. Adjust the temperature to 200ºC and air fry for 8 minutes. 4. After 5 minutes, flip over the cheese mixture. 5. Allow to cool 5 minutes before cutting into sticks. Serve warm.

Garlic Dill Wings

Prep time: 5 minutes | Cook time: 25 minutes | Serves 4

900 g bone-in chicken wings,
separated at joints
½ teaspoon salt
½ teaspoon ground black

pepper
½ teaspoon onion powder
½ teaspoon garlic powder
1 teaspoon dried dill

1. In a large bowl, toss wings with salt, pepper, onion powder, garlic powder, and dill until evenly coated. Place wings into ungreased air fryer basket in a single layer, working in batches if needed. 2. Adjust the temperature to 200ºC and air fry for 25 minutes, shaking the basket every 7 minutes during cooking. Wings should have an internal temperature of at least 76ºC and be golden brown when done. Serve warm.

Chicken Drumsticks with Barbecue-Honey Sauce

Prep time: 5 minutes | Cook time: 40 minutes | Serves 5

1 tablespoon olive oil
10 chicken drumsticks
Chicken seasoning or rub, to taste

Salt and ground black pepper, to taste
240 ml barbecue sauce
85 g honey

1. Preheat the air fryer to 200ºC. Grease the air fryer basket with olive oil. 2. Rub the chicken drumsticks with chicken seasoning or rub, salt and ground black pepper on a clean work surface. 3. Arrange the chicken drumsticks in a single layer in the air fryer, then air fry for 18 minutes or until lightly browned. Flip the drumsticks halfway through. You may need to work in batches to avoid overcrowding. 4. Meanwhile, combine the barbecue sauce and honey in a small bowl. Stir to mix well. 5. Remove the drumsticks from the air fryer and baste with the sauce mixture to serve.

Italian Chicken with Sauce

Prep time: 15 minutes | Cook time: 20 minutes | Serves 4

2 large skinless chicken breasts
(about 565 g)
Salt and freshly ground black
pepper
50 g almond meal
45 g grated Parmesan cheese
2 teaspoons Italian seasoning

1 egg, lightly beaten
1 tablespoon olive oil
225 g no-sugar-added marinara
sauce
4 slices Mozzarella cheese or
110 g shredded Mozzarella

1. Preheat the air fryer to 180ºC. 2. Slice the chicken breasts in half horizontally to create 4 thinner chicken breasts. Working with one piece at a time, place the chicken between two pieces of parchment paper and pound with a meat mallet or rolling pin to flatten to an even thickness. Season both sides with salt and freshly ground black pepper. 3. In a large shallow bowl, combine the almond meal, Parmesan, and Italian seasoning; stir until thoroughly combined. Place the egg in another large shallow bowl. 4. Dip the chicken in the egg, followed by the almond meal mixture, pressing the mixture firmly into the chicken to create an even coating. 5. Working in batches if necessary, arrange the chicken breasts in a single layer in the air fryer basket and coat both sides lightly with olive oil. Pausing halfway through the cooking time to flip the chicken, air fry for 15 minutes, or until a thermometer inserted into the thickest part registers 76ºC. 6. Spoon the marinara sauce over each piece of chicken and top with the Mozzarella cheese. Air fry for an additional 3 to 5 minutes until the cheese is melted.

African Merguez Meatballs

Prep time: 30 minutes | Cook time: 10 minutes | Serves 4

450 g chicken mince
2 garlic cloves, finely minced
1 tablespoon sweet Hungarian
paprika
1 teaspoon kosher salt
1 teaspoon sugar

1 teaspoon ground cumin
½ teaspoon black pepper
½ teaspoon ground fennel
½ teaspoon ground coriander
½ teaspoon cayenne pepper
¼ teaspoon ground allspice

1. In a large bowl, gently mix the chicken, garlic, paprika, salt, sugar, cumin, black pepper, fennel, coriander, cayenne, and allspice until all the ingredients are incorporated. Let stand for 30 minutes at room temperature, or cover and refrigerate for up to 24 hours. 2. Form the mixture into 16 meatballs. Arrange them in a single layer in the air fryer basket. Set the air fryer to 200ºC for 10 minutes, turning the meatballs halfway through the cooking time. Use a meat thermometer to ensure the meatballs have reached an internal temperature of 76ºC.

Teriyaki Chicken Thighs with Lemony Snow Peas

Prep time: 30 minutes | Cook time: 34 minutes | Serves 4

60 ml chicken broth
½ teaspoon grated fresh ginger
⅛ teaspoon red pepper flakes
1½ tablespoons soy sauce
4 (140 g) bone-in chicken thighs, trimmed
1 tablespoon mirin
½ teaspoon cornflour

1 tablespoon sugar
170 g mangetout, strings removed
⅛ teaspoon lemon zest
1 garlic clove, minced
¼ teaspoon salt
Ground black pepper, to taste
½ teaspoon lemon juice

1. Combine the broth, ginger, pepper flakes, and soy sauce in a large bowl. Stir to mix well. 2. Pierce 10 to 15 holes into the chicken skin. Put the chicken in the broth mixture and toss to coat well. Let sit for 10 minutes to marinate. 3. Preheat the air fryer to 206°C. 4. Transfer the marinated chicken on a plate and pat dry with paper towels. 5. Scoop 2 tablespoons of marinade in a microwave-safe bowl and combine with mirin, cornflour and sugar. Stir to mix well. Microwave for 1 minute or until frothy and has a thick consistency. Set aside. 6. Arrange the chicken in the preheated air fryer, skin side up, and air fry for 25 minutes or until the internal temperature of the chicken reaches at least 76°C. Gently turn the chicken over halfway through. 7. When the frying is complete, brush the chicken skin with marinade mixture. Air fryer the chicken for 5 more minutes or until glazed. 8. Remove the chicken from the air fryer and reserve ½ teaspoon of chicken fat remains in the air fryer. Allow the chicken to cool for 10 minutes. 9. Meanwhile, combine the reserved chicken fat, snow peas, lemon zest, garlic, salt, and ground black pepper in a small bowl. Toss to coat well. 10. Transfer the snow peas in the air fryer and air fry for 3 minutes or until soft. Remove the peas from the air fryer and toss with lemon juice. 11. Serve the chicken with lemony snow peas.

Ethiopian Chicken with Cauliflower

Prep time: 15 minutes | Cook time: 28 minutes | Serves 6

2 handful fresh Italian parsley, roughly chopped
20 g fresh chopped chives
2 sprigs thyme
6 chicken drumsticks
1½ small-sized head cauliflower, broken into large-sized florets
2 teaspoons mustard powder

⅓ teaspoon porcini powder
1½ teaspoons berbere spice
⅓ teaspoon sweet paprika
½ teaspoon shallot powder
1 teaspoon granulated garlic
1 teaspoon freshly cracked pink peppercorns
½ teaspoon sea salt

1. Simply combine all items for the berbere spice rub mix. After that, coat the chicken drumsticks with this rub mix on all sides. Transfer them to the baking dish. 2. Now, lower the cauliflower onto the chicken drumsticks. Add thyme, chives and Italian parsley and spritz everything with a pan spray. Transfer the baking dish to the preheated air fryer. 3. Next step, set the timer for 28 minutes; roast at 180°C, turning occasionally. Bon appétit!

Hawaiian Chicken Bites

Prep time: 1 hour 15 minutes | Cook time: 15 minutes | Serves 4

120 ml pineapple juice
2 tablespoons apple cider vinegar
½ tablespoon minced ginger
120 g ketchup
2 garlic cloves, minced

110 g brown sugar
2 tablespoons sherry
120 ml soy sauce
4 chicken breasts, cubed
Cooking spray

1. Combine the pineapple juice, cider vinegar, ginger, ketchup, garlic, and sugar in a saucepan. Stir to mix well. Heat over low heat for 5 minutes or until thickened. Fold in the sherry and soy sauce. 2. Dunk the chicken cubes in the mixture. Press to submerge. Wrap the bowl in plastic and refrigerate to marinate for at least an hour. 3. Preheat the air fryer to 180°C. Spritz the air fryer basket with cooking spray. 4. Remove the chicken cubes from the marinade. Shake the excess off and put in the preheated air fryer. Spritz with cooking spray. 5. Air fry for 15 minutes or until the chicken cubes are glazed and well browned. Shake the basket at least three times during the frying. 6. Serve immediately.

Sweet and Spicy Turkey Meatballs

Prep time: 15 minutes | Cook time: 15 minutes | Serves 6

Olive oil
450 g lean turkey mince
60 g whole-wheat panko bread crumbs
1 egg, beaten
1 tablespoon soy sauce
60 ml plus 1 tablespoon hoisin

sauce, divided
2 teaspoons minced garlic
⅛ teaspoon salt
⅛ teaspoon freshly ground black pepper
1 teaspoon Sriracha

1. Spray the air fryer basket lightly with olive oil. 2. In a large bowl, mix together the turkey, panko bread crumbs, egg, soy sauce, 1 tablespoon of hoisin sauce, garlic, salt, and black pepper. 3. Using a tablespoon, form 24 meatballs. 4. In a small bowl, combine the remaining 60 ml of hoisin sauce and Sriracha to make a glaze and set aside. 5. Place the meatballs in the air fryer basket in a single layer. You may need to cook them in batches. 6. Air fry at 180°C for 8 minutes. Brush the meatballs generously with the glaze and cook until cooked through, an additional 4 to 7 minutes.

Teriyaki Chicken Legs

Prep time: 12 minutes | Cook time: 18 to 20 minutes | Serves 2

4 tablespoons teriyaki sauce
1 tablespoon orange juice
1 teaspoon smoked paprika

4 chicken legs
Cooking spray

1. Mix together the teriyaki sauce, orange juice, and smoked paprika. Brush on all sides of chicken legs. 2. Spray the air fryer basket with nonstick cooking spray and place chicken in basket. 3. Air fry at 180ºC for 6 minutes. Turn and baste with sauce. Cook for 6 more minutes, turn and baste. Cook for 6 to 8 minutes more, until juices run clear when chicken is pierced with a fork.

Coconut Chicken Meatballs

Prep time: 10 minutes | Cook time: 14 minutes | Serves 4

450 g chicken mince
2 spring onions, finely chopped
20 g chopped fresh corinader leaves
20 g unsweetened shredded coconut
1 tablespoon hoisin sauce

1 tablespoon soy sauce
2 teaspoons Sriracha or other hot sauce
1 teaspoon toasted sesame oil
½ teaspoon kosher salt
1 teaspoon black pepper

1. In a large bowl, gently mix the chicken, spring onions, coriander, coconut, hoisin, soy sauce, Sriracha, sesame oil, salt, and pepper until thoroughly combined (the mixture will be wet and sticky). 2. Place a sheet of parchment paper in the air fryer basket. Using a small scoop or teaspoon, drop rounds of the mixture in a single layer onto the parchment paper. 3. Set the air fryer to 180ºC for 10 minutes, turning the meatballs halfway through the cooking time. Raise the air fryer temperature to 200ºC and cook for 4 minutes more to brown the outsides of the meatballs. Use a meat thermometer to ensure the meatballs have reached an internal temperature of 76ºC. 4. Transfer the meatballs to a serving platter. Repeat with any remaining chicken mixture.

Fajita Chicken Strips

Prep time: 10 minutes | Cook time: 15 minutes | Serves 4

450 g boneless, skinless chicken tenderloins, cut into strips
3 bell peppers, any color, cut into chunks
1 onion, cut into chunks

1 tablespoon olive oil
1 tablespoon fajita seasoning mix
Cooking spray

1. Preheat the air fryer to 190ºC. 2. In a large bowl, mix together the chicken, bell peppers, onion, olive oil, and fajita seasoning mix until completely coated. 3. Spray the air fryer basket lightly with cooking spray. 4. Place the chicken and vegetables in the air fryer basket and lightly spray with cooking spray. 5. Air fry for 7 minutes. Shake the basket and air fry for an additional 5 to 8 minutes, until the chicken is cooked through and the veggies are starting to char. 6. Serve warm.

Stuffed Chicken Florentine

Prep time: 10 minutes | Cook time: 20 minutes | Serves 4

3 tablespoons pine nuts
40 g frozen spinach, thawed and squeezed dry
75 g ricotta cheese
2 tablespoons grated Parmesan cheese
3 cloves garlic, minced

Salt and freshly ground black pepper, to taste
4 small boneless, skinless chicken breast halves (about 680 g)
8 slices bacon

1. Place the pine nuts in a small pan and set in the air fryer basket. Set the air fryer to 200ºC and air fry for 2 to 3 minutes until toasted. Remove the pine nuts to a mixing bowl and continue preheating the air fryer. 2. In a large bowl, combine the spinach, ricotta, Parmesan, and garlic. Season to taste with salt and pepper and stir well until thoroughly combined. 3. Using a sharp knife, cut into the chicken breasts, slicing them across and opening them up like a book, but be careful not to cut them all the way through. Sprinkle the chicken with salt and pepper. 4. Spoon equal amounts of the spinach mixture into the chicken, then fold the top of the chicken breast back over the top of the stuffing. Wrap each chicken breast with 2 slices of bacon. 5. Working in batches if necessary, air fry the chicken for 18 to 20 minutes until the bacon is crisp and a thermometer inserted into the thickest part of the chicken registers 76ºC.

Lemon-Basil Turkey Breasts

Prep time: 30 minutes | Cook time: 58 minutes | Serves 4

2 tablespoons olive oil
900 g turkey breasts, bone-in, skin-on
Coarse sea salt and ground black pepper, to taste

1 teaspoon fresh basil leaves, chopped
2 tablespoons lemon zest, grated

1. Rub olive oil on all sides of the turkey breasts; sprinkle with salt, pepper, basil, and lemon zest. 2. Place the turkey breasts skin side up on the parchment-lined air fryer basket. 3. Cook in the preheated air fryer at 170ºC for 30 minutes. Now, turn them over and cook an additional 28 minutes. 4. Serve with lemon wedges, if desired. Bon appétit!

Garlic Soy Chicken Thighs

Prep time: 10 minutes | Cook time: 30 minutes | Serves 1 to 2

2 tablespoons chicken stock
2 tablespoons reduced-sodium soy sauce
1½ tablespoons sugar
4 garlic cloves, smashed and peeled

2 large spring onions, cut into 2- to 3-inch batons, plus more, thinly sliced, for garnish
2 bone-in, skin-on chicken thighs (198 to 225 g each)

1. Preheat the air fryer to 190°C. 2. In a metal cake pan, combine the chicken stock, soy sauce, and sugar and stir until the sugar dissolves. Add the garlic cloves, spring onions, and chicken thighs, turning the thighs to coat them in the marinade, then resting them skin-side up. Place the pan in the air fryer and bake, flipping the thighs every 5 minutes after the first 10 minutes, until the chicken is cooked through and the marinade is reduced to a sticky glaze over the chicken, about 30 minutes. 3. Remove the pan from the air fryer and serve the chicken thighs warm, with any remaining glaze spooned over top and sprinkled with more sliced spring onions.

Chicken and Avocado Fajitas

Prep time: 10 minutes | Cook time: 10 to 14 minutes | Serves 4

Cooking oil spray
4 boneless, skinless chicken breasts, sliced crosswise
1 small red onion, sliced
2 red bell peppers, seeded and sliced
120 ml spicy ranch salad

dressing, divided
½ teaspoon dried oregano
8 corn tortillas
40 g torn butter lettuce leaves
2 avocados, peeled, pitted, and chopped

1. Insert the crisper plate into the basket and the basket into the unit. Preheat the unit by selecting BAKE, setting the temperature to 190°C, and setting the time to 3 minutes. Select START/STOP to begin. 2. Once the unit is preheated, spray the crisper plate with cooking oil. Place the chicken, red onion, and red bell pepper into the basket. Drizzle with 1 tablespoon of the salad dressing and season with the oregano. Toss to combine. 3. Select BAKE, set the temperature to 190°C, and set the time to 14 minutes. Select START/STOP to begin. 4. After 10 minutes, check the chicken. If a food thermometer inserted into the chicken registers at least 76°C, it is done. If not, resume cooking. 5. When the cooking is complete, transfer the chicken and vegetables to a bowl and toss with the remaining salad dressing. 6. Serve the chicken mixture family-style with the tortillas, lettuce, and avocados, and let everyone make their own plates.

Chicken Hand Pies

Prep time: 30 minutes | Cook time: 10 minutes per batch | Makes 8 pies

180 ml chicken broth
130 g frozen mixed peas and carrots
140 g cooked chicken, chopped
1 tablespoon cornflour

1 tablespoon milk
Salt and pepper, to taste
1 (8-count) can organic flaky biscuits
Oil for misting or cooking spray

1. In a medium saucepan, bring chicken broth to a boil. Stir in the frozen peas and carrots and cook for 5 minutes over medium heat. Stir in chicken. 2. Mix the cornflour into the milk until it dissolves. Stir it into the simmering chicken broth mixture and cook just until thickened. 3. Remove from heat, add salt and pepper to taste, and let cool slightly. 4. Lay biscuits out on wax paper. Peel each biscuit apart in the middle to make 2 rounds so you have 16 rounds total. Using your hands or a rolling pin, flatten each biscuit round slightly to make it larger and thinner. 5. Divide chicken filling among 8 of the biscuit rounds. Place remaining biscuit rounds on top and press edges all around. Use the tines of a fork to crimp biscuit edges and make sure they are sealed well. 6. Spray both sides lightly with oil or cooking spray. 7. Cook in a single layer, 4 at a time, at 170°C for 10 minutes or until biscuit dough is cooked through and golden brown.

Classic Whole Chicken

Prep time: 5 minutes | Cook time: 50 minutes | Serves 4

Oil, for spraying
1 (1.8 kg) whole chicken, giblets removed
1 tablespoon olive oil
1 teaspoon paprika
½ teaspoon granulated garlic

½ teaspoon salt
½ teaspoon freshly ground black pepper
¼ teaspoon finely chopped fresh parsley, for garnish

1. Line the air fryer basket with parchment and spray lightly with oil. 2. Pat the chicken dry with paper towels. Rub it with the olive oil until evenly coated. 3. In a small bowl, mix together the paprika, garlic, salt, and black pepper and sprinkle it evenly over the chicken. 4. Place the chicken in the prepared basket, breast-side down. 5. Air fry at 180°C for 30 minutes, flip, and cook for another 20 minutes, or until the internal temperature reaches 76°C and the juices run clear. 6. Sprinkle with the parsley before serving.

Cheesy Pepperoni and Chicken Pizza

Prep time: 15 minutes | Cook time: 15 minutes | Serves 6

280 g cooked chicken, cubed
240 g pizza sauce
20 slices pepperoni

20 g grated Parmesan cheese
225 g shredded Mozzarella cheese
Cooking spray

1. Preheat the air fryer to 190ºC. Spritz a baking pan with cooking spray. 2. Arrange the chicken cubes in the prepared baking pan, then top the cubes with pizza sauce and pepperoni. Stir to coat the cubes and pepperoni with sauce. 3. Scatter the cheeses on top, then place the baking pan in the preheated air fryer. Air fryer for 15 minutes or until frothy and the cheeses melt. 4. Serve immediately.

Chapter 6 Vegetables and Sides

Parmesan-Rosemary Radishes

Prep time: 5 minutes | Cook time: 15 to 20 minutes | Serves 4

1 bunch radishes, stemmed, trimmed, and quartered
1 tablespoon avocado oil
2 tablespoons finely grated fresh Parmesan cheese
1 tablespoon chopped fresh rosemary
Sea salt and freshly ground black pepper, to taste

1. Place the radishes in a medium bowl and toss them with the avocado oil, Parmesan cheese, rosemary, salt, and pepper. 2. Set the air fryer to192°C. Arrange the radishes in a single layer in the air fryer basket. Roast for 15 to 20 minutes, until golden brown and tender. Let cool for 5 minutes before serving.

Cauliflower with Lime Juice

Prep time: 10 minutes | Cook time: 7 minutes | Serves 4

215 g chopped cauliflower florets
2 tablespoons coconut oil, melted
2 teaspoons chili powder
½ teaspoon garlic powder
1 medium lime
2 tablespoons chopped coriander

1. In a large bowl, toss cauliflower with coconut oil. Sprinkle with chili powder and garlic powder. Place seasoned cauliflower into the air fryer basket. 2. Adjust the temperature to 180°C and set the timer for 7 minutes. 3. Cauliflower will be tender and begin to turn golden at the edges. Place into a serving bowl. 4. Cut the lime into quarters and squeeze juice over cauliflower. Garnish with coriander.

Roasted Brussels Sprouts with Orange and Garlic

Prep time: 5 minutes | Cook time: 10 minutes | Serves 4

450 g Brussels sprouts, quartered
2 garlic cloves, minced
2 tablespoons olive oil
½ teaspoon salt
1 orange, cut into rings

1. Preheat the air fryer to 180°C. 2. In a large bowl, toss the quartered Brussels sprouts with the garlic, olive oil, and salt until well coated. 3. Pour the Brussels sprouts into the air fryer, lay the orange slices on top of them, and roast for 10 minutes. 4. Remove from the air fryer and set the orange slices aside. Toss the Brussels sprouts before serving.

Golden Garlicky Mushrooms

Prep time: 10 minutes | Cook time: 10 minutes | Serves 4

6 small mushrooms
1 tablespoon bread crumbs
1 tablespoon olive oil
30 g onion, peeled and diced
1 teaspoon parsley
1 teaspoon garlic purée
Salt and ground black pepper, to taste

1. Preheat the air fryer to 180°C. 2. Combine the bread crumbs, oil, onion, parsley, salt, pepper and garlic in a bowl. Cut out the mushrooms' stalks and stuff each cap with the crumb mixture. 3. Air fry in the air fryer for 10 minutes. 4. Serve hot.

Chermoula-Roasted Beetroots

Prep time: 15 minutes | Cook time: 25 minutes | Serves 4

Chermoula:
30 g packed fresh coriander leaves
15 g packed fresh parsley leaves
6 cloves garlic, peeled
2 teaspoons smoked paprika
2 teaspoons ground cumin
1 teaspoon ground coriander
½ to 1 teaspoon cayenne pepper
Pinch crushed saffron (optional)
115 ml extra-virgin olive oil
coarse sea salt, to taste
Beetroots:
3 medium beetroots, trimmed, peeled, and cut into 1-inch chunks
2 tablespoons chopped fresh coriander
2 tablespoons chopped fresh parsley

1. For the chermoula: In a food processor, combine the fresh coriander, parsley, garlic, paprika, cumin, ground coriander, and cayenne. Pulse until coarsely chopped. Add the saffron, if using, and process until combined. With the food processor running, slowly add the olive oil in a steady stream; process until the sauce is uniform. Season to taste with salt. 2. For the beetroots: In a large bowl, drizzle the beetroots with ½ cup of the chermoula, or enough to coat. Arrange the beetroots in the air fryer basket. Set the air fryer to 192°C for 25 to minutes, or until the beetroots are tender. 3. Transfer the beetroots to a serving platter. Sprinkle with chopped coriander and parsley and serve.

Tahini-Lemon Kale

Prep time: 5 minutes | Cook time: 15 minutes | Serves 2 to 4

60 g tahini
60 ml fresh lemon juice
2 tablespoons olive oil
1 teaspoon sesame seeds
½ teaspoon garlic powder
¼ teaspoon cayenne pepper

110 g packed torn kale leaves (stems and ribs removed and leaves torn into palm-size pieces)
coarse sea salt and freshly ground black pepper, to taste

1. In a large bowl, whisk together the tahini, lemon juice, olive oil, sesame seeds, garlic powder, and cayenne until smooth. Add the kale leaves, season with salt and black pepper, and toss in the dressing until completely coated. Transfer the kale leaves to a cake pan. 2. Place the pan in the air fryer and roast at 180°C, stirring every 5 minutes, until the kale is wilted and the top is lightly browned, about 15 minutes. Remove the pan from the air fryer and serve warm.

Saltine Wax Beans

Prep time: 10 minutes | Cook time: 7 minutes | Serves 4

60 g flour
1 teaspoon smoky chipotle powder
½ teaspoon ground black pepper

1 teaspoon sea salt flakes
2 eggs, beaten
55 g crushed cream crackers
285 g wax beans
Cooking spray

1. Preheat the air fryer to 180°C. 2. Combine the flour, chipotle powder, black pepper, and salt in a bowl. Put the eggs in a second bowl. Put the crushed cream crackers in a third bowl. 3. Wash the beans with cold water and discard any tough strings. 4. Coat the beans with the flour mixture, before dipping them into the beaten egg. Cover them with the crushed cream crackers. 5. Spritz the beans with cooking spray. 6. Air fry for 4 minutes. Give the air fryer basket a good shake and continue to air fry for 3 minutes. Serve hot.

Bacon-Wrapped Asparagus

Prep time: 10 minutes | Cook time: 10 minutes | Serves 4

8 slices reduced-sodium bacon, cut in half
16 thick (about 450 g) asparagus spears, trimmed of woody ends

1. Preheat the air fryer to 180°C. 2. Wrap a half piece of bacon around the centre of each stalk of asparagus. 3. Working in batches, if necessary, arrange seam-side down in a single layer in the air fryer basket. Air fry for 10 minutes until the bacon is crisp and the stalks are tender.

Parmesan and Herb Sweet Potatoes

Prep time: 10 minutes | Cook time: 18 minutes | Serves 4

2 large sweet potatoes, peeled and cubed
65 ml olive oil
1 teaspoon dried rosemary

½ teaspoon salt
2 tablespoons shredded Parmesan

1. Preheat the air fryer to 180°C. 2. In a large bowl, toss the sweet potatoes with the olive oil, rosemary, and salt. 3. Pour the potatoes into the air fryer basket and roast for 10 minutes, then stir the potatoes and sprinkle the Parmesan over the top. Continue roasting for 8 minutes more. 4. Serve hot and enjoy.

Sweet-and-Sour Brussels Sprouts

Prep time: 10 minutes | Cook time: 20 minutes | Serves 2

70 g Thai sweet chili sauce
2 tablespoons black vinegar or balsamic vinegar
½ teaspoon hot sauce, such as Tabasco
230 g Brussels sprouts, trimmed (large sprouts halved)

2 small shallots, cut into ¼-inch-thick slices
coarse sea salt and freshly ground black pepper, to taste
2 teaspoons lightly packed fresh coriander leaves

1. In a large bowl, whisk together the chili sauce, vinegar, and hot sauce. Add the Brussels sprouts and shallots, season with salt and pepper, and toss to combine. Scrape the Brussels sprouts and sauce into a cake pan. 2. Place the pan in the air fryer and roast at 192°C, stirring every 5 minutes, until the Brussels sprouts are tender and the sauce is reduced to a sticky glaze, about 20 minutes. 3. Remove the pan from the air fryer and transfer the Brussels sprouts to plates. Sprinkle with the coriander and serve warm.

Dinner Rolls

Prep time: 10 minutes | Cook time: 12 minutes | Serves 6

225 g shredded Mozzarella cheese
30 g full-fat cream cheese
95 g blanched finely ground

almond flour
40 g ground flaxseed
½ teaspoon baking powder
1 large egg

1. Place Mozzarella, cream cheese, and almond flour in a large microwave-safe bowl. Microwave for 1 minute. Mix until smooth. 2. Add flaxseed, baking powder, and egg until fully combined and smooth. Microwave an additional 15 seconds if it becomes too firm. 3. Separate the dough into six pieces and roll into balls. Place the balls into the air fryer basket. 4. Adjust the temperature to 160°C and air fry for 12 minutes. 5. Allow rolls to cool completely before serving.

Roasted Potatoes and Asparagus

Prep time: 5 minutes | Cook time: 23 minutes | Serves 4

4 medium potatoes
1 bunch asparagus
75 g cottage cheese
80 g low-fat crème fraiche

1 tablespoon wholegrain
mustard
Salt and pepper, to taste
Cooking spray

1. Preheat the air fryer to 200°C. Spritz the air fryer basket with cooking spray. 2. Place the potatoes in the basket. Air fry the potatoes for 20 minutes. 3. Boil the asparagus in salted water for 3 minutes. 4. Remove the potatoes and mash them with rest of ingredients. Sprinkle with salt and pepper. 5. Serve immediately.

Courgette Fritters

Prep time: 10 minutes | Cook time: 10 minutes | Serves 4

2 courgette, grated (about 450 g)
1 teaspoon salt
25 g almond flour
20 g grated Parmesan cheese
1 large egg

¼ teaspoon dried thyme
¼ teaspoon ground turmeric
¼ teaspoon freshly ground black pepper
1 tablespoon olive oil
½ lemon, sliced into wedges

1. Preheat the air fryer to 200°C. Cut a piece of parchment paper to fit slightly smaller than the bottom of the air fryer. 2. Place the courgette in a large colander and sprinkle with the salt. Let sit for 5 to 10 minutes. Squeeze as much liquid as you can from the courgette and place in a large mixing bowl. Add the almond flour, Parmesan, egg, thyme, turmeric, and black pepper. Stir gently until thoroughly combined. 3. Shape the mixture into 8 patties and arrange on the parchment paper. Brush lightly with the olive oil. Pausing halfway through the cooking time to turn the patties, air fry for 10 minutes until golden brown. Serve warm with the lemon wedges.

Turnip Fries

Prep time: 10 minutes | Cook time: 20 to 30 minutes | Serves 4

900 g turnip, peeled and cut into ¼ to ½-inch fries
2 tablespoons olive oil

Salt and freshly ground black pepper, to taste

1. Preheat the air fryer to 200°C. 2. In a large bowl, combine the turnip and olive oil. Season to taste with salt and black pepper. Toss gently until thoroughly coated. 3. Working in batches if necessary, spread the turnip in a single layer in the air fryer basket. Pausing halfway through the cooking time to shake the basket, air fry for 20 to 30 minutes until the fries are lightly browned and crunchy.

Green Peas with Mint

Prep time: 5 minutes | Cook time: 5 minutes | Serves 4

75 g shredded lettuce
1 (280 g) package frozen green peas, thawed

1 tablespoon fresh mint, shredded
1 teaspoon melted butter

1. Lay the shredded lettuce in the air fryer basket. 2. Toss together the peas, mint, and melted butter and spoon over the lettuce. 3. Air fry at 180°C for 5 minutes, until peas are warm and lettuce wilts.

Herbed Shiitake Mushrooms

Prep time: 10 minutes | Cook time: 5 minutes | Serves 4

230 g shiitake mushrooms, stems removed and caps roughly chopped
1 tablespoon olive oil
½ teaspoon salt
Freshly ground black pepper, to taste

1 teaspoon chopped fresh thyme leaves
1 teaspoon chopped fresh oregano
1 tablespoon chopped fresh parsley

1. Preheat the air fryer to 200°C. 2. Toss the mushrooms with the olive oil, salt, pepper, thyme and oregano. Air fry for 5 minutes, shaking the basket once or twice during the cooking process. The mushrooms will still be somewhat chewy with a meaty texture. If you'd like them a little more tender, add a couple of minutes to this cooking time. 3. Once cooked, add the parsley to the mushrooms and toss. Season again to taste and serve.

Crispy Courgette Sticks

Prep time: 5 minutes | Cook time: 14 minutes | Serves 4

2 small courgette, cut into 2-inch × ½-inch sticks
3 tablespoons chickpea flour
2 teaspoons arrowroot (or cornflour)
½ teaspoon garlic granules

¼ teaspoon sea salt
⅛ teaspoon freshly ground black pepper
1 tablespoon water
Cooking spray

1. Preheat the air fryer to 200°C. 2. Combine the courgette sticks with the chickpea flour, arrowroot, garlic granules, salt, and pepper in a medium bowl and toss to coat. Add the water and stir to mix well. 3. Spritz the air fryer basket with cooking spray and spread out the courgette sticks in the basket. Mist the courgette sticks with cooking spray. 4. Air fry for 14 minutes, shaking the basket halfway through, or until the courgette sticks are crispy and nicely browned. 5. Serve warm.

Tamarind Sweet Potatoes

Prep time: 5 minutes | Cook time: 20 to 25 minutes | Serves 4

5 garnet sweet potatoes, peeled and diced
1½ tablespoons fresh lime juice
1 tablespoon butter, melted
2 teaspoons tamarind paste

1½ teaspoon ground allspice
⅓ teaspoon white pepper
½ teaspoon turmeric powder
A few drops liquid stevia

1. Preheat the air fryer to 200ºC. 2. In a large mixing bowl, combine all the ingredients and toss until the sweet potatoes are evenly coated. 3. Place the sweet potatoes in the air fryer basket and air fry for 20 t0 25 minutes, or until the potatoes are crispy on the outside and soft on the inside. Shake the basket twice during cooking. 4. Let the potatoes cool for 5 minutes before serving.

Spicy Roasted Bok Choy

Prep time: 10 minutes | Cook time: 7 to 10 minutes | Serves 4

2 tablespoons olive oil
2 tablespoons reduced-sodium coconut aminos
2 teaspoons sesame oil
2 teaspoons chili-garlic sauce

2 cloves garlic, minced
1 head (about 450 g) bok choy, sliced lengthwise into quarters
2 teaspoons black sesame seeds

1. Preheat the air fryer to 200ºC. 2. In a large bowl, combine the olive oil, coconut aminos, sesame oil, chili-garlic sauce, and garlic. Add the bok choy and toss, massaging the leaves with your hands if necessary, until thoroughly coated. 3. Arrange the bok choy in the basket of the air fryer. Pausing about halfway through the cooking time to shake the basket, air fry for 7 to 10 minutes until the bok choy is tender and the tips of the leaves begin to crisp. 4.Remove from the basket and let cool for a few minutes before coarsely chopping. Serve sprinkled with the sesame seeds.

Fried Brussels Sprouts

Prep time: 10 minutes | Cook time: 18 minutes | Serves 4

1 teaspoon plus 1 tablespoon extra-virgin olive oil, divided
2 teaspoons minced garlic
2 tablespoons honey
1 tablespoon sugar
2 tablespoons freshly squeezed lemon juice
2 tablespoons rice vinegar

2 tablespoons sriracha
450 g Brussels sprouts, stems trimmed and any tough leaves removed, rinsed, halved lengthwise, and dried
½ teaspoon salt
Cooking oil spray

1. In a small saucepan over low heat, combine 1 teaspoon of olive oil, the garlic, honey, sugar, lemon juice, vinegar, and sriracha. Cook for 2 to 3 minutes, or until slightly thickened. Remove the pan from the heat, cover, and set aside. 2. Place the Brussels sprouts in a resealable bag or small bowl. Add the remaining olive oil and the salt, and toss to coat. 3. Insert the crisper plate into the basket and the basket into the unit. Preheat the unit by selecting AIR FRY, setting the temperature to 200ºC, and setting the time to 3 minutes. Select START/STOP to begin. 4. Once the unit is preheated, spray the crisper plate with cooking oil. Add the Brussels sprouts to the basket. 5. Select AIR FRY, set the temperature to 200ºC, and set the time to 15 minutes. Select START/STOP to begin. 6. After 7 or 8 minutes, remove the basket and shake it to toss the sprouts. Reinsert the basket to resume cooking. 7. When the cooking is complete, the leaves should be crispy and light brown and the sprout centres tender. 8. Place the sprouts in a medium serving bowl and drizzle the sauce over the top. Toss to coat, and serve immediately.

Spinach and Sweet Pepper Poppers

Prep time: 10 minutes | Cook time: 8 minutes | Makes 16 poppers

110 g cream cheese, softened
20 g chopped fresh spinach leaves
½ teaspoon garlic powder

8 mini sweet bell peppers, tops removed, seeded, and halved lengthwise

1. In a medium bowl, mix cream cheese, spinach, and garlic powder. Place 1 tablespoon mixture into each sweet pepper half and press down to smooth. 2. Place poppers into ungreased air fryer basket. Adjust the temperature to 200ºC and air fry for 8 minutes. Poppers will be done when cheese is browned on top and peppers are tender-crisp. Serve warm.

Cheese-Walnut Stuffed Mushrooms

Prep time: 5 minutes | Cook time: 10 minutes | Serves 4

4 large portobello mushrooms
1 tablespoon rapeseed oil
110 g shredded Mozzarella cheese

35 g minced walnuts
2 tablespoons chopped fresh parsley
Cooking spray

1. Preheat the air fryer to 180ºC. Spritz the air fryer basket with cooking spray. 2. On a clean work surface, remove the mushroom stems. Scoop out the gills with a spoon and discard. Coat the mushrooms with rapeseed oil. Top each mushroom evenly with the shredded Mozzarella cheese, followed by the minced walnuts. 3. Arrange the mushrooms in the air fryer and roast for 10 minutes until golden brown. 4. Transfer the mushrooms to a plate and sprinkle the parsley on top for garnish before serving.

Simple Cougette Crisps

Prep time: 5 minutes | Cook time: 14 minutes | Serves 4

2 courgette, sliced into ¼- to ½-inch-thick rounds	Freshly ground black pepper, to taste (optional)
¼ teaspoon garlic granules	Cooking spray
⅛ teaspoon sea salt	

1. Preheat the air fryer to 200°C. Spritz the air fryer basket with cooking spray. 2. Put the courgette rounds in the air fryer basket, spreading them out as much as possible. Top with a sprinkle of garlic granules, sea salt, and black pepper (if desired). Spritz the courgette rounds with cooking spray. 3. Roast for 14 minutes, flipping the courgette rounds halfway through, or until the courgette rounds are crisp-tender. 4. Let them rest for 5 minutes and serve.

Asian-Inspired Roasted Broccoli

Prep time: 10 minutes | Cook time: 15 minutes | Serves 4

Broccoli:	Sauce:
Oil, for spraying	2 tablespoons soy sauce
450 g broccoli florets	2 teaspoons honey
2 teaspoons peanut oil	2 teaspoons Sriracha
1 tablespoon minced garlic	1 teaspoon rice vinegar
½ teaspoon salt	

Make the Broccoli 1. Line the air fryer basket with parchment and spray lightly with oil. 2. In a large bowl, toss together the broccoli, peanut oil, garlic, and salt until evenly coated. 3. Spread out the broccoli in an even layer in the prepared basket. 4. Air fry at 200°C for 15 minutes, stirring halfway through. Make the Sauce 5. Meanwhile, in a small microwave-safe bowl, combine the soy sauce, honey, Sriracha, and rice vinegar and microwave on high for about 15 seconds. Stir to combine. 6. Transfer the broccoli to a serving bowl and add the sauce. Gently toss until evenly coated and serve immediately.

Green Tomato Salad

Prep time: 10 minutes | Cook time: 8 to 10 minutes | Serves 4

4 green tomatoes	2 teaspoons fresh lemon juice
½ teaspoon salt	2 tablespoons finely chopped fresh parsley
1 large egg, lightly beaten	
50 g peanut flour	1 teaspoon dried dill
1 tablespoon Creole seasoning	1 teaspoon dried chives
1 (140 g) bag rocket	½ teaspoon salt
Buttermilk Dressing:	½ teaspoon garlic powder
230 g mayonnaise	½ teaspoon onion powder
120 g sour cream	

1. Preheat the air fryer to 200°C. 2. Slice the tomatoes into ½-inch slices and sprinkle with the salt. Let sit for 5 to 10 minutes. 3. Place the egg in a small shallow bowl. In another small shallow bowl, combine the peanut flour and Creole seasoning. Dip each tomato slice into the egg wash, then dip into the peanut flour mixture, turning to coat evenly. 4. Working in batches if necessary, arrange the tomato slices in a single layer in the air fryer basket and spray both sides lightly with olive oil. Air fry until browned and crisp, 8 to 10 minutes. 5. To make the buttermilk dressing: In a small bowl, whisk together the mayonnaise, sour cream, lemon juice, parsley, dill, chives, salt, garlic powder, and onion powder. 6. Serve the tomato slices on top of a bed of the rocket with the dressing on the side.

Fried Courgette Salad

Prep time: 10 minutes | Cook time: 5 to 7 minutes | Serves 4

2 medium courgette, thinly sliced	Zest and juice of ½ lemon
5 tablespoons olive oil, divided	1 clove garlic, minced
15 g chopped fresh parsley	65 g crumbled feta cheese
2 tablespoons chopped fresh mint	Freshly ground black pepper, to taste

1. Preheat the air fryer to 200°C. 2. In a large bowl, toss the courgette slices with 1 tablespoon of the olive oil. 3. Working in batches if necessary, arrange the courgette slices in an even layer in the air fryer basket. Pausing halfway through the cooking time to shake the basket, air fry for 5 to 7 minutes until soft and lightly browned on each side. 4. Meanwhile, in a small bowl, combine the remaining 4 tablespoons olive oil, parsley, mint, lemon zest, lemon juice, and garlic. 5. Arrange the courgette on a plate and drizzle with the dressing. Sprinkle the feta and black pepper on top. Serve warm or at room temperature.

Mushrooms with Goat Cheese

Prep time: 10 minutes | Cook time: 10 minutes | Serves 4

3 tablespoons vegetable oil	½ teaspoon black pepper
450 g mixed mushrooms, trimmed and sliced	110 g goat cheese, diced
1 clove garlic, minced	2 teaspoons chopped fresh thyme leaves (optional)
¼ teaspoon dried thyme	

1. In a baking pan, combine the oil, mushrooms, garlic, dried thyme, and pepper. Stir in the goat cheese. Place the pan in the air fryer basket. Set the air fryer to 200°C for 10 minutes, stirring halfway through the cooking time. 2. Sprinkle with fresh thyme, if desired.

Polenta Casserole

Prep time: 5 minutes | Cook time: 28 to 30 minutes | Serves 4

10 fresh asparagus spears, cut into 1-inch pieces

320 g cooked polenta, cooled to room temperature

1 egg, beaten

2 teaspoons Worcestershire sauce

½ teaspoon garlic powder

¼ teaspoon salt

2 slices emmental cheese (about 40 g)

Oil for misting or cooking spray

1. Mist asparagus spears with oil and air fry at 200ºC for 5 minutes, until crisp-tender. 2. In a medium bowl, mix together the grits, egg, Worcestershire, garlic powder, and salt. 3. Spoon half of polenta mixture into a baking pan and top with asparagus. 4. Tear cheese slices into pieces and layer evenly on top of asparagus. 5. Top with remaining polenta. 6. Bake at 180ºC for 23 to 25 minutes. The casserole will rise a little as it cooks. When done, the top will have browned lightly with just a hint of crispiness.

"Faux-Tato" Hash

Prep time: 10 minutes | Cook time: 12 minutes | Serves 4

450 g radishes, ends removed, quartered

¼ medium yellow onion, peeled and diced

½ medium green pepper, seeded and chopped

2 tablespoons salted butter, melted

½ teaspoon garlic powder

¼ teaspoon ground black pepper

1. In a large bowl, combine radishes, onion, and bell pepper. Toss with butter. 2. Sprinkle garlic powder and black pepper over mixture in bowl, then spoon into ungreased air fryer basket. 3. Adjust the temperature to 160ºC and air fry for 12 minutes. Shake basket halfway through cooking. Radishes will be tender when done. Serve warm.

Citrus Sweet Potatoes and Carrots

Prep time: 5 minutes | Cook time: 20 to 25 minutes | Serves 4

2 large carrots, cut into 1-inch chunks

1 medium sweet potato, peeled and cut into 1-inch cubes

25 g chopped onion

2 garlic cloves, minced

2 tablespoons honey

1 tablespoon freshly squeezed orange juice

2 teaspoons butter, melted

1. Insert the crisper plate into the basket and the basket into the unit. Preheat the unit by selecting AIR ROAST, setting the temperature to 200ºC, and setting the time to 3 minutes. Select START/STOP to begin. 2. In a 6-by-2-inch round pan, toss together the carrots, sweet potato, onion, garlic, honey, orange juice, and melted butter to coat. 3. Once the unit is preheated, place the pan into the basket. 4. Select AIR ROAST, set the temperature to 200ºC, and set the time to 25 minutes. Select START/STOP to begin. 5. After 15 minutes, remove the basket and shake the vegetables. Reinsert the basket to resume cooking. After 5 minutes, if the vegetables are tender and glazed, they are done. If not, resume cooking. 6. When the cooking is complete, serve immediately.

Chapter 7 Vegetarian Mains

Vegetable Burgers

Prep time: 10 minutes | Cook time: 12 minutes | Serves 4

227 g cremini or chestnut mushrooms
2 large egg yolks
½ medium courgette, trimmed and chopped
60 ml peeled and chopped
brown onion
1 clove garlic, peeled and finely minced
½ teaspoon salt
¼ teaspoon ground black pepper

Place all ingredients into a food processor and pulse twenty times until finely chopped and combined. Separate mixture into four equal sections and press each into a burger shape. Place burgers into ungreased air fryer basket. Adjust the temperature to 192°C and air fry for 12 minutes, turning burgers halfway through cooking. Burgers will be browned and firm when done. Place burgers on a large plate and let cool 5 minutes before serving.

Sweet Pepper Nachos

Prep time: 10 minutes | Cook time: 5 minutes | Serves 2

6 mini sweet peppers, seeded and sliced in half
180 ml shredded Colby jack or Monterey Jack cheese
60 ml sliced pickled jalapeños
½ medium avocado, peeled, pitted, and diced
2 tablespoons sour cream

Place peppers into an ungreased round non-stick baking dish. Sprinkle with cheese and top with jalapeños. Place dish into air fryer basket. Adjust the temperature to 176°C and bake for 5 minutes. Cheese will be melted and bubbly when done. Remove dish from air fryer and top with avocado. Drizzle with sour cream. Serve warm.

Quiche-Stuffed Peppers

Prep time: 5 minutes | Cook time: 15 minutes | Serves 2

2 medium green peppers
3 large eggs
60 ml full-fat ricotta cheese
60 ml diced brown onion
120 ml chopped broccoli
120 ml shredded medium Cheddar cheese

Cut the tops off of the peppers and remove the seeds and white membranes with a small knife. In a medium bowl, whisk eggs and ricotta. Add onion and broccoli. Pour the egg and vegetable mixture evenly into each pepper. Top with Cheddar. Place peppers into a 1 L round baking dish and place into the air fryer basket. Adjust the temperature to 176°C and bake for 15 minutes. Eggs will be mostly firm and peppers tender when fully cooked. Serve immediately.

Sweet Potatoes with Courgette

Prep time: 20 minutes | Cook time: 20 minutes | Serves 4

2 large-sized sweet potatoes, peeled and quartered
1 medium courgette, sliced
1 Serrano or jalapeño pepper, deseeded and thinly sliced
1 pepper, deseeded and thinly sliced
1 to 2 carrots, cut into matchsticks
60 ml olive oil
1½ tablespoons maple syrup
½ teaspoon porcini powder or paste
¼ teaspoon mustard powder
½ teaspoon fennel seeds
1 tablespoon garlic powder
½ teaspoon fine sea salt
¼ teaspoon ground black pepper
Tomato ketchup, for serving

Put the sweet potatoes, courgette, peppers, and the carrot into the air fryer basket. Coat with a drizzling of olive oil. Preheat the air fryer to 176°C. Air fry the vegetables for 15 minutes. In the meantime, prepare the sauce by vigorously combining the other ingredients, except for the tomato ketchup, with a whisk. Lightly grease a baking dish. Transfer the cooked vegetables to the baking dish, pour over the sauce and coat the vegetables well. Increase the temperature to 200°C and air fry the vegetables for an additional 5 minutes. Serve warm with a side of ketchup.

Cheese Stuffed Peppers

Prep time: 20 minutes | Cook time: 15 minutes | Serves 2

1 red pepper, top and seeds removed
1 yellow pepper, top and seeds removed
Salt and pepper, to taste
235 ml Cottage cheese
4 tablespoons mayonnaise
2 pickles, chopped

Arrange the peppers in the lightly greased air fryer basket. Cook in the preheated air fryer at 204°C for 15 minutes, turning them over halfway through the cooking time. Season with salt and pepper. Then, in a mixing bowl, combine the soft white cheese with the mayonnaise and chopped pickles. Stuff the pepper with the soft white cheese mixture and serve. Enjoy!

Tangy Asparagus and Broccoli

Prep time: 25 minutes | Cook time: 22 minutes | Serves 4

230 g asparagus, cut into 1½-inch pieces
230 g broccoli, cut into 1½-inch pieces
2 tablespoons olive oil

Salt and white pepper, to taste
120 ml vegetable broth
2 tablespoons apple cider vinegar

Place the vegetables in a single layer in the lightly greased air fryer basket. Drizzle the olive oil over the vegetables. Sprinkle with salt and white pepper. Cook at 192°C for 15 minutes, shaking the basket halfway through the cooking time. Add 120 ml of vegetable broth to a saucepan; bring to a rapid boil and add the vinegar. Cook for 5 to 7 minutes or until the sauce has reduced by half. Spoon the sauce over the warm vegetables and serve immediately. Bon appétit!

Roasted Vegetables with Rice

Prep time: 5 minutes | Cook time: 12 minutes | Serves 4

2 teaspoons melted butter
235 ml chopped mushrooms
235 ml cooked rice
235 ml peas
1 carrot, chopped

1 red onion, chopped
1 garlic clove, minced
Salt and black pepper, to taste
2 hard-boiled eggs, grated
1 tablespoon soy sauce

Preheat the air fryer to 192°C. Coat a baking dish with melted butter. Stir together the mushrooms, cooked rice, peas, carrot, onion, garlic, salt, and pepper in a large bowl until well mixed. Pour the mixture into the prepared baking dish and transfer to the air fryer basket. Roast in the preheated air fryer for 12 minutes until the vegetables are tender. Divide the mixture among four plates. Serve warm with a sprinkle of grated eggs and a drizzle of soy sauce.

Spaghetti Squash Alfredo

Prep time: 10 minutes | Cook time: 15 minutes | Serves 2

½ large cooked spaghetti squash
2 tablespoons salted butter, melted
120 ml low-carb Alfredo sauce
60 ml grated vegetarian Parmesan cheese

½ teaspoon garlic powder
1 teaspoon dried parsley
¼ teaspoon ground peppercorn
120 ml shredded Italian blend cheese

Using a fork, remove the strands of spaghetti squash from the shell. Place into a large bowl with butter and Alfredo sauce. Sprinkle with Parmesan, garlic powder, parsley, and peppercorn. Pour into a 1 L round baking dish and top with shredded cheese. Place dish into the air fryer basket. Adjust the temperature to 160°C and bake for 15 minutes. When finished, cheese will be golden and bubbling. Serve immediately.

Crustless Spinach Cheese Pie

Prep time: 10 minutes | Cook time: 20 minutes | Serves 4

6 large eggs
60 ml double cream
235 ml frozen chopped spinach, drained

235 ml shredded sharp Cheddar cheese
60 ml diced brown onion

In a medium bowl, whisk eggs and add cream. Add remaining ingredients to bowl. Pour into a round baking dish. Place into the air fryer basket. Adjust the temperature to 160°C and bake for 20 minutes. Eggs will be firm and slightly browned when cooked. Serve immediately.

Broccoli Crust Pizza

Prep time: 15 minutes | Cook time: 12 minutes | Serves 4

700 ml riced broccoli, steamed and drained well
1 large egg
120 ml grated vegetarian Parmesan cheese

3 tablespoons low-carb Alfredo sauce
120 ml shredded Mozzarella cheese

In a large bowl, mix broccoli, egg, and Parmesan. Cut a piece of parchment to fit your air fryer basket. Press out the pizza mixture to fit on the parchment, working in two batches if necessary. Place into the air fryer basket. Adjust the temperature to 188°C and air fry for 5 minutes. The crust should be firm enough to flip. If not, add 2 additional minutes. Flip crust. Top with Alfredo sauce and Mozzarella. Return to the air fryer basket and cook an additional 7 minutes or until cheese is golden and bubbling. Serve warm.

Crispy Cabbage Steaks

Prep time: 5 minutes | Cook time: 10 minutes | Serves 4

1 small head green cabbage, cored and cut into ½-inch-thick slices
¼ teaspoon salt
¼ teaspoon ground black pepper

2 tablespoons olive oil
1 clove garlic, peeled and finely minced
½ teaspoon dried thyme
½ teaspoon dried parsley

Sprinkle each side of cabbage with salt and pepper, then place into ungreased air fryer basket, working in batches if needed. Drizzle each side of cabbage with olive oil, then sprinkle with remaining ingredients on both sides. Adjust the temperature to 176°C and air fry for 10 minutes, turning "steaks" halfway through cooking. 3.Cabbage will be browned at the edges and tender when done. Serve warm.

Baked Turnip and Courgette

Prep time: 5 minutes | Cook time: 15 to 20 minutes | Serves 4

3 turnips, sliced
1 large courgette, sliced
1 large red onion, cut into rings

2 cloves garlic, crushed
1 tablespoon olive oil
Salt and black pepper, to taste

Preheat the air fryer to 166°C. Put the turnips, courgette, red onion, and garlic in a baking pan. Drizzle the olive oil over the top and sprinkle with the salt and pepper. Place the baking pan in the preheated air fryer and bake for 15 to 20 minutes, or until the vegetables are tender. Remove from the basket and serve on a plate.

Lush Summer Rolls

Prep time: 15 minutes | Cook time: 15 minutes | Serves 4

235 ml shiitake mushroom, sliced thinly
1 celery stalk, chopped
1 medium carrot, shredded
½ teaspoon finely chopped ginger
1 teaspoon sugar

1 tablespoon soy sauce
1 teaspoon Engevita yeast flakes
8 spring roll sheets
1 teaspoon corn starch
2 tablespoons water

In a bowl, combine the ginger, soy sauce, Engevita yeast flakes, carrots, celery, mushroom, and sugar. Mix the cornflour and water to create an adhesive for the spring rolls. Scoop a tablespoonful of the vegetable mixture into the middle of the spring roll sheets. Brush the edges of the sheets with the cornflour adhesive and enclose around the filling to make spring rolls. Preheat the air fryer to 204°C. When warm, place the rolls inside and air fry for 15 minutes or until crisp. Serve hot.

Garlicky Sesame Carrots

Prep time: 5 minutes | Cook time: 16 minutes | Serves 4 to 6

450 g baby carrots
1 tablespoon sesame oil
½ teaspoon dried dill
Pinch salt

Freshly ground black pepper, to taste
6 cloves garlic, peeled
3 tablespoons sesame seeds

Preheat the air fryer to 192°C. In a medium bowl, drizzle the baby carrots with the sesame oil. Sprinkle with the dill, salt, and pepper and toss to coat well. Place the baby carrots in the air fryer basket and roast for 8 minutes. Remove the basket and stir in the garlic. Return the basket to the air fryer and roast for another 8 minutes, or until the carrots are lightly browned. Serve sprinkled with the sesame seeds.

Broccoli-Cheese Fritters

Prep time: 5 minutes | Cook time: 20 to 25 minutes | Serves 4

235 ml broccoli florets
235 ml shredded Mozzarella cheese
180 ml almond flour
120 ml milled flaxseed, divided
2 teaspoons baking powder

1 teaspoon garlic powder
Salt and freshly ground black pepper, to taste
2 eggs, lightly beaten
120 ml ranch dressing

Preheat the air fryer to 204°C. In a food processor fitted with a metal blade, pulse the broccoli until very finely chopped. Transfer the broccoli to a large bowl and add the Mozzarella, almond flour, 60 ml milled flaxseed, baking powder, and garlic powder. Stir until thoroughly combined. Season to taste with salt and black pepper. Add the eggs and stir again to form a sticky dough. Shape the dough into 1¼-inch fritters. Place the remaining 60 ml milled flaxseed in a shallow bowl and roll the fritters in the meal to form an even coating. Working in batches if necessary, arrange the fritters in a single layer in the basket of the air fryer and spray generously with olive oil. Pausing halfway through the cooking time to shake the basket, air fry for 20 to 25 minutes until the fritters are golden brown and crispy. Serve with the ranch dressing for dipping.

Cauliflower Steak with Gremolata

Prep time: 15 minutes | Cook time: 25 minutes | Serves 4

2 tablespoons olive oil
1 tablespoon Italian seasoning
1 large head cauliflower, outer leaves removed and sliced lengthwise through the core into thick "steaks"
Salt and freshly ground black pepper, to taste

60 ml Parmesan cheese
Gremolata:
1 bunch Italian parsley
2 cloves garlic
Zest of 1 small lemon, plus 1 to 2 teaspoons lemon juice
120 ml olive oil
Salt and pepper, to taste

Preheat the air fryer to 204°C. In a small bowl, combine the olive oil and Italian seasoning. Brush both sides of each cauliflower "steak" generously with the oil. Season to taste with salt and black pepper. Working in batches if necessary, arrange the cauliflower in a single layer in the air fryer basket. Pausing halfway through the cooking time to turn the "steaks," air fry for 15 to 20 minutes until the cauliflower is tender and the edges begin to brown. Sprinkle with the Parmesan and air fry for 5 minutes longer. To make the gremolata: In a food processor fitted with a metal blade, combine the parsley, garlic, and lemon zest and juice. With the motor running, add the olive oil in a steady stream until the mixture forms a bright green sauce. Season to taste with salt and black pepper. Serve the cauliflower steaks with the gremolata spooned over the top.

Super Veg Rolls

Prep time: 20 minutes | Cook time: 10 minutes | Serves 6

2 potatoes, mashed
60 ml peas
60 ml mashed carrots
1 small cabbage, sliced
60 ml beans
2 tablespoons sweetcorn

1 small onion, chopped
120 ml breadcrumbs
1 packet spring roll sheets
120 ml cornflour slurry (mix 40 ml cornflour with 80 ml water)

Preheat the air fryer to 200ºC. Boil all the vegetables in water over a low heat. Rinse and allow to dry. Unroll the spring roll sheets and spoon equal amounts of vegetable onto the centre of each one. Fold into spring rolls and coat each one with the slurry and breadcrumbs. Air fry the rolls in the preheated air fryer for 10 minutes. Serve warm.

Potato and Broccoli with Tofu Scramble

Prep time: 15 minutes | Cook time: 30 minutes | Serves 3

600 ml chopped red potato
2 tablespoons olive oil, divided
1 block tofu, chopped finely
2 tablespoons tamari
1 teaspoon turmeric powder

½ teaspoon onion powder
½ teaspoon garlic powder
120 ml chopped onion
1 L broccoli florets

Preheat the air fryer to 204ºC. Toss together the potatoes and 1 tablespoon of the olive oil. Air fry the potatoes in a baking dish for 15 minutes, shaking once during the cooking time to ensure they fry evenly. Combine the tofu, the remaining 1 tablespoon of the olive oil, turmeric, onion powder, tamari, and garlic powder together, stirring in the onions, followed by the broccoli. Top the potatoes with the tofu mixture and air fry for an additional 15 minutes. Serve warm.

Stuffed Portobellos

Prep time: 10 minutes | Cook time: 8 minutes | Serves 4

85 g soft white cheese
½ medium courgette, trimmed and chopped
60 ml seeded and chopped red pepper
350 ml chopped fresh spinach

leaves
4 large portobello mushrooms, stems removed
2 tablespoons coconut oil, melted
½ teaspoon salt

In a medium bowl, mix soft white cheese, courgette, pepper, and spinach. Drizzle mushrooms with coconut oil and sprinkle with salt. Scoop ¼ courgette mixture into each mushroom. Place mushrooms into ungreased air fryer basket. Adjust the temperature to 204ºC and air fry for 8 minutes. Portobellos will be tender, and tops will be browned when done. Serve warm.

Basmati Risotto

Prep time: 10 minutes | Cook time: 30 minutes | Serves 2

1 onion, diced
1 small carrot, diced
475 ml vegetable broth, boiling
120 ml grated Cheddar cheese

1 clove garlic, minced
180 ml long-grain basmati rice
1 tablespoon olive oil
1 tablespoon unsalted butter

Preheat the air fryer to 200ºC. Grease a baking tin with oil and stir in the butter, garlic, carrot, and onion. Put the tin in the air fryer and bake for 4 minutes. Pour in the rice and bake for a further 4 minutes, stirring three times throughout the baking time. Turn the temperature down to 160ºC. Add the vegetable broth and give the dish a gentle stir. Bake for 22 minutes, leaving the air fryer uncovered. Pour in the cheese, stir once more and serve.

Air Fryer Veggies with Halloumi

Prep time: 5 minutes | Cook time: 14 minutes | Serves 2

2 courgettes, cut into even chunks
1 large aubergine, peeled, cut into chunks
1 large carrot, cut into chunks

170 g halloumi cheese, cubed
2 teaspoons olive oil
Salt and black pepper, to taste
1 teaspoon dried mixed herbs

Preheat the air fryer to 172ºC. Combine the courgettes, aubergine, carrot, cheese, olive oil, salt, and pepper in a large bowl and toss to coat well. Spread the mixture evenly in the air fryer basket and air fry for 14 minutes until crispy and golden, shaking the basket once during cooking. Serve topped with mixed herbs.

Super Vegetable Burger

Prep time: 15 minutes | Cook time: 12 minutes | Serves 8

230 g cauliflower, steamed and diced, rinsed and drained
2 teaspoons coconut oil, melted
2 teaspoons minced garlic
60 ml desiccated coconut
120 ml oats
3 tablespoons flour
1 tablespoon flaxseeds plus 3

tablespoons water, divided
1 teaspoon mustard powder
2 teaspoons thyme
2 teaspoons parsley
2 teaspoons chives
Salt and ground black pepper, to taste
235 ml breadcrumbs

Preheat the air fryer to 200ºC. Combine the cauliflower with all the ingredients, except for the breadcrumbs, incorporating everything well. Using the hands, shape 8 equal-sized amounts of the mixture into burger patties. Coat the patties in breadcrumbs before putting them in the air fryer basket in a single layer. Air fry for 12 minutes or until crispy. Serve hot.

Cheese Stuffed Courgette

Prep time: 20 minutes | Cook time: 8 minutes | Serves 4

1 large courgette, cut into four pieces	parsley, roughly chopped
2 tablespoons olive oil	1 heaping tablespoon coriander, minced
235 ml Ricotta cheese, room temperature	60 g Cheddar cheese, preferably freshly grated
2 tablespoons spring onions, chopped	1 teaspoon celery seeds
	½ teaspoon salt
1 heaping tablespoon fresh	½ teaspoon garlic pepper

Cook your courgette in the air fryer basket for approximately 10 minutes at 176°C. Check for doneness and cook for 2-3 minutes longer if needed. Meanwhile, make the stuffing by mixing the other items. When your courgette is thoroughly cooked, open them up. Divide the stuffing among all courgette pieces and bake an additional 5 minutes.

Crispy Aubergine Rounds

Prep time: 15 minutes | Cook time: 10 minutes | Serves 4

1 large aubergine, ends trimmed, cut into ½-inch slices	crisps, finely ground
½ teaspoon salt	½ teaspoon paprika
60 g Parmesan 100% cheese	¼ teaspoon garlic powder
	1 large egg

Sprinkle aubergine rounds with salt. Place rounds on a kitchen towel for 30 minutes to draw out excess water. Pat rounds dry. In a medium bowl, mix cheese crisps, paprika, and garlic powder. In a separate medium bowl, whisk egg. Dip each aubergine round in egg, then gently press into cheese crisps to coat both sides. Place aubergine rounds into ungreased air fryer basket. Adjust the temperature to 204°C and air fry for 10 minutes, turning rounds halfway through cooking. Aubergine will be golden and crispy when done. Serve warm.

Rosemary Beetroots with Balsamic Glaze

Prep time: 5 minutes | Cook time: 10 minutes | Serves 2

Beetroot:	Salt and black pepper, to taste
2 beetroots, cubed	Balsamic Glaze:
2 tablespoons olive oil	80 ml balsamic vinegar
2 sprigs rosemary, chopped	1 tablespoon honey

Preheat the air fryer to 204°C. Combine the beetroots, olive oil, rosemary, salt, and pepper in a mixing bowl and toss until the beetroots are completely coated. Place the beetroots in the air fryer basket and air fry for 10 minutes until the beetroots are crisp and browned at the edges. Shake the basket halfway through the cooking time. Meanwhile, make the balsamic glaze: Place the balsamic vinegar and honey in a small saucepan and bring to a boil over medium heat. When the sauce starts to boil, reduce the heat to medium-low heat and simmer until the liquid is reduced by half. When ready, remove the beetroots from the basket to a platter. Pour the balsamic glaze over the top and serve immediately.

Cayenne Tahini Kale

Prep time: 5 minutes | Cook time: 15 minutes | Serves 2 to 4

Dressing:	Kale:
60 ml tahini	1 L packed torn kale leaves (stems and ribs removed and leaves torn into palm-size pieces)
60 ml fresh lemon juice	
2 tablespoons olive oil	
1 teaspoon sesame seeds	
½ teaspoon garlic powder	Rock salt and freshly ground black pepper, to taste
¼ teaspoon cayenne pepper	

Preheat the air fryer to 176°C. Make the dressing: Whisk together the tahini, lemon juice, olive oil, sesame seeds, garlic powder, and cayenne pepper in a large bowl until well mixed. Add the kale and massage the dressing thoroughly all over the leaves. Sprinkle the salt and pepper to season. Place the kale in the air fryer basket in a single layer and air fry for about 15 minutes, or until the leaves are slightly wilted and crispy. Remove from the basket and serve on a plate.

Crispy Tofu

Prep time: 30 minutes | Cook time: 15 to 20 minutes | Serves 4

1 (454 g) block extra-firm tofu	1 tablespoon chilli-garlic sauce
2 tablespoons coconut aminos	1½ teaspoons black sesame seeds
1 tablespoon toasted sesame oil	
1 tablespoon olive oil	1 spring onion, thinly sliced

Press the tofu for at least 15 minutes by wrapping it in paper towels and setting a heavy pan on top so that the moisture drains. Slice the tofu into bite-size cubes and transfer to a bowl. Drizzle with the coconut aminos, sesame oil, olive oil, and chilli-garlic sauce. Cover and refrigerate for 1 hour or up to overnight. Preheat the air fryer to 204°C. Arrange the tofu in a single layer in the air fryer basket. Pausing to shake the pan halfway through the cooking time, air fry for 15 to 20 minutes until crisp. Serve with any juices that accumulate in the bottom of the air fryer, sprinkled with the sesame seeds and sliced spring onion.

Spinach Cheese Casserole

Prep time: 15 minutes | Cook time: 15 minutes | Serves 4

1 tablespoon salted butter, melted
60 ml diced brown onion
227 g full fat soft white cheese
80 ml full-fat mayonnaise
80 ml full-fat sour cream

60 ml chopped pickled jalapeños
475 ml fresh spinach, chopped
475 ml cauliflower florets, chopped
235 ml artichoke hearts, chopped

In a large bowl, mix butter, onion, soft white cheese, mayonnaise, and sour cream. Fold in jalapeños, spinach, cauliflower, and artichokes. Pour the mixture into a round baking dish. Cover with foil and place into the air fryer basket. Adjust the temperature to 188°C and set the timer for 15 minutes. In the last 2 minutes of cooking, remove the foil to brown the top. Serve warm.

Gold Ravioli

Prep time: 10 minutes | Cook time: 6 minutes | Serves 4

120 ml panko breadcrumbs
2 teaspoons Engevita yeast flakes
1 teaspoon dried basil
1 teaspoon dried oregano
1 teaspoon garlic powder

Salt and ground black pepper, to taste
60 ml aquafaba or egg alternative
227 g ravioli
Cooking spray

Cover the air fryer basket with aluminium foil and coat with a light brushing of oil. Preheat the air fryer to 204°C. Combine the panko breadcrumbs, Engevita yeast flakes, basil, oregano, and garlic powder. Sprinkle with salt and pepper to taste. Put the aquafaba in a separate bowl. Dip the ravioli in the aquafaba before coating it in the panko mixture. Spritz with cooking spray and transfer to the air fryer. Air fry for 6 minutes. Shake the air fryer basket halfway. Serve hot.

Crispy Aubergine Slices with Parsley

Prep time: 5 minutes | Cook time: 10 to 12 minutes | Serves 4

235 ml flour
4 eggs
Salt, to taste
475 ml breadcrumbs
1 teaspoon Italian seasoning

2 aubergines, sliced
2 garlic cloves, sliced
2 tablespoons chopped parsley
Cooking spray

Preheat the air fryer to 200°C. Spritz the air fryer basket with cooking spray. On a plate, place the flour. In a shallow bowl, whisk the eggs with salt. In another shallow bowl, combine the breadcrumbs and Italian seasoning. Dredge the aubergine slices, one at a time, in the flour, then in the whisked eggs, finally in the bread crumb mixture to coat well. Arrange the coated aubergine slices in the air fryer basket and air fry for 10 to 12 minutes until golden brown and crispy. Flip the aubergine slices halfway through the cooking time. Transfer the aubergine slices to a plate and sprinkle the garlic and parsley on top before serving.

Chapter 8 Desserts

Simple Apple Turnovers

Prep time: 10 minutes | Cook time: 10 minutes | Serves 4

1 apple, peeled, quartered, and thinly sliced
½ teaspoons pumpkin pie spice
Juice of ½ lemon
1 tablespoon granulated sugar
Pinch of kosher, or coarse sea salt
6 sheets filo pastry

1. Preheat the air fryer to 164°C. 2. In a medium bowl, combine the apple, pumpkin pie spice, lemon juice, granulated sugar, and kosher salt. 3. Cut the filo pastry sheets into 4 equal pieces and place individual tablespoons of apple filling in the center of each piece, then fold in both sides and roll from front to back. 4. Spray the air fryer basket with nonstick cooking spray, then place the turnovers in the basket and bake for 10 minutes or until golden brown. 5. Remove the turnovers from the air fryer and allow to cool on a wire rack for 10 minutes before serving.

Coconut Muffins

Prep time: 5 minutes | Cook time: 25 minutes | Serves 5

55 g coconut flour
2 tablespoons cocoa powder
3 tablespoons granulated sweetener
1 teaspoon baking powder
2 tablespoons coconut oil
2 eggs, beaten
50 g desiccated coconut

1. In the mixing bowl, mix all ingredients. 2. Then pour the mixture into the molds of the muffin and transfer in the air fryer basket. 3. Cook the muffins at 176°C for 25 minutes.

Bourbon Bread Pudding

Prep time: 10 minutes | Cook time: 20 minutes | Serves 4

3 slices whole grain bread, cubed
1 large egg
240 ml whole milk
2 tablespoons bourbon, or peach juice
½ teaspoons vanilla extract
4 tablespoons maple syrup, divided
½ teaspoons ground cinnamon
2 teaspoons sparkling sugar

1. Preheat the air fryer to 132°C. 2. Spray a baking pan with nonstick cooking spray, then place the bread cubes in the pan. 3. In a medium bowl, whisk together the egg, milk, bourbon, vanilla extract, 3 tablespoons of maple syrup, and cinnamon. Pour the egg mixture over the bread and press down with a spatula to coat all the bread, then sprinkle the sparkling sugar on top and bake for 20 minutes. 4. Remove the pudding from the air fryer and allow to cool in the pan on a wire rack for 10 minutes. Drizzle the remaining 1 tablespoon of maple syrup on top. Slice and serve warm.

Chocolate Cake

Prep time: 10 minutes | Cook time: 20 to 23 minutes | Serves 8

100 g granulated sugar
30 g plain flour, plus 3 tablespoons
3 tablespoons cocoa
½ teaspoon baking powder
½ teaspoon baking soda
¼ teaspoon salt
1 egg
2 tablespoons oil
120 ml milk
½ teaspoon vanilla extract

1. Preheat the air fryer to 164°C. 2. Grease and flour a baking pan. 3. In a medium bowl, stir together the sugar, flour, cocoa, baking powder, baking soda, and salt. 4. Add all other ingredients and beat with a wire whisk until smooth. 5. Pour batter into prepared pan and bake for 20 to 23 minutes, until toothpick inserted in center comes out clean, or with crumbs clinging to it.

Baked Brazilian Pineapple

Prep time: 10 minutes | Cook time: 10 minutes | Serves 4

95 g brown sugar
2 teaspoons ground cinnamon
1 small pineapple, peeled,
cored, and cut into spears
3 tablespoons unsalted butter, melted

1. In a small bowl, mix the brown sugar and cinnamon until thoroughly combined. 2. Brush the pineapple spears with the melted butter. Sprinkle the cinnamon-sugar over the spears, pressing lightly to ensure it adheres well. 3. Place the spears in the air fryer basket in a single layer. (Depending on the size of your air fryer, you may have to do this in batches.) Set the air fryer to 204°C and cook for 10 minutes for the first batch (6 to 8 minutes for the next batch, as the fryer will be preheated). Halfway through the cooking time, brush the spears with butter. 4. The pineapple spears are done when they are heated through, and the sugar is bubbling. Serve hot.

Pineapple Wontons

Prep time: 15 minutes | Cook time: 15 to 18 minutes per batch | Serves 5

225 g cream cheese	20 wonton wrappers
170 g finely chopped fresh pineapple	Cooking oil spray

1. In a small microwave-safe bowl, heat the cream cheese in the microwave on high power for 20 seconds to soften. 2. In a medium bowl, stir together the cream cheese and pineapple until mixed well. 3. Lay out the wonton wrappers on a work surface. A clean table or large cutting board works well. 4. Spoon 1½ teaspoons of the cream cheese mixture onto each wrapper. Be careful not to overfill. 5. Fold each wrapper diagonally across to form a triangle. Bring the 2 bottom corners up toward each other. Do not close the wrapper yet. Bring up the 2 open sides and push out any air. Squeeze the open edges together to seal. 6. Insert the crisper plate into the basket and the basket into the unit. Preheat the air fryer to 200°C. 7. Once the unit is preheated, spray the crisper plate with cooking oil. Place the wontons into the basket. You can work in batches or stack the wontons. Spray the wontons with the cooking oil. 8. Cook wontons for 10 minutes, then remove the basket, flip each wonton, and spray them with more oil. Reinsert the basket to resume cooking for 5 to 8 minutes more until the wontons are light golden brown and crisp. 9. If cooking in batches, remove the cooked wontons from the basket and repeat steps 7 and 8 for the remaining wontons. 10. When the cooking is complete, cool for 5 minutes before serving.

Blackberry Peach Cobbler with Vanilla

Prep time: 10 minutes | Cook time: 20 minutes | Serves 4

Filling:	1 tablespoon maple syrup
170 g blackberries	1 teaspoon vanilla
250 g chopped peaches, cut into	3 tablespoons coconut sugar
½-inch thick slices	40 g rolled oats
2 teaspoons arrowroot or cornflour	45 g whole-wheat pastry, or plain flour
2 tablespoons coconut sugar	1 teaspoon cinnamon
1 teaspoon lemon juice	¼ teaspoon nutmeg
Topping:	⅛ teaspoon sea salt
2 tablespoons sunflower oil	

Make the Filling: 1. Combine the blackberries, peaches, arrowroot, coconut sugar, and lemon juice in a baking pan. 2. Using a rubber spatula, stir until well incorporated. Set aside. Make the Topping: 3. Preheat the air fryer to 162°C 4. Combine the oil, maple syrup, and vanilla in a mixing bowl and stir well. Whisk in the remaining ingredients. Spread this mixture evenly over the filling. 5. Place the pan in the air fryer basket and bake for 20 minutes, or until the topping is crispy and golden brown. Serve warm

Glazed Cherry Turnovers

Prep time: 10 minutes | Cook time: 14 minutes per batch | Serves 8

2 sheets frozen puff pastry, thawed	1 egg, beaten
	90 g sliced almonds
600 g can premium cherry pie filling	120 g icing sugar
	2 tablespoons milk
2 teaspoons ground cinnamon	

1. Roll a sheet of puff pastry out into a square that is approximately 10-inches by 10-inches. Cut this large square into quarters. 2. Mix the cherry pie filling and cinnamon together in a bowl. Spoon ¼ cup of the cherry filling into the center of each puff pastry square. Brush the perimeter of the pastry square with the egg wash. Fold one corner of the puff pastry over the cherry pie filling towards the opposite corner, forming a triangle. Seal the two edges of the pastry together with the tip of a fork, making a design with the tines. Brush the top of the turnovers with the egg wash and sprinkle sliced almonds over each one. Repeat these steps with the second sheet of puff pastry. You should have eight turnovers at the end. 3. Preheat the air fryer to 188°C. 4. Air fry two turnovers at a time for 14 minutes, carefully turning them over halfway through the cooking time. 5. While the turnovers are cooking, make the glaze by whisking the icing sugar and milk together in a small bowl until smooth. Let the glaze sit for a minute so the sugar can absorb the milk. If the consistency is still too thick to drizzle, add a little more milk, a drop at a time, and stir until smooth. 6. Let the cooked cherry turnovers sit for at least 10 minutes. Then drizzle the glaze over each turnover in a zigzag motion. Serve warm or at room temperature.

Butter Flax Cookies

Prep time: 25 minutes | Cook time: 20 minutes | Serves 4

225 g almond meal	A pinch of coarse salt
2 tablespoons flaxseed meal	1 large egg, room temperature.
30 g monk fruit, or equivalent sweetener	110 g unsalted butter, room temperature
1 teaspoon baking powder	1 teaspoon vanilla extract
A pinch of grated nutmeg	

1. Mix the almond meal, flaxseed meal, monk fruit, baking powder, grated nutmeg, and salt in a bowl. 2. In a separate bowl, whisk the egg, butter, and vanilla extract. 3. Stir the egg mixture into dry mixture; mix to combine well or until it forms a nice, soft dough. 4. Roll your dough out and cut out with a cookie cutter of your choice. Bake in the preheated air fryer at 176°C for 10 minutes. Decrease the temperature to 164°C and cook for 10 minutes longer. Bon appétit!

Roasted Honey Pears

Prep time: 7 minutes | Cook time: 18 to 23 minutes | Serves 4

2 large Bosc pears, halved lengthwise and seeded
3 tablespoons honey
1 tablespoon unsalted butter

½ teaspoon ground cinnamon
30 g walnuts, chopped
55 g part-skim ricotta cheese, divided

1. Insert the crisper plate into the basket and the basket into the unit. Preheat to 176°C. 2. In a 6-by-2-inch round pan, place the pears cut-side up. 3. In a small microwave-safe bowl, melt the honey, butter, and cinnamon. Brush this mixture over the cut sides of the pears. Pour 3 tablespoons of water around the pears in the pan. 4. Once the unit is preheated, place the pan into the basket. 5. After about 18 minutes, check the pears. They should be tender when pierced with a fork and slightly crisp on the edges. If not, resume cooking. 6. When the cooking is complete, baste the pears once with the liquid in the pan. Carefully remove the pears from the pan and place on a serving plate. Drizzle each with some liquid from the pan, sprinkle the walnuts on top, and serve with a spoonful of ricotta cheese.

Molten Chocolate Almond Cakes

Prep time: 5 minutes | Cook time: 13 minutes | Serves 3

Butter and flour for the ramekins
110 g bittersweet chocolate, chopped
110 gunsalted butter
2 eggs
2 egg yolks
50 g granulated sugar
½ teaspoon pure vanilla extract,

or almond extract
1 tablespoon plain flour
3 tablespoons ground almonds
8 to 12 semisweet chocolate discs (or 4 chunks of chocolate)
Cocoa powder or icing sugar, for dusting
Toasted almonds, coarsely chopped

1. Butter and flour three (170 g) ramekins. (Butter the ramekins and then coat the butter with flour by shaking it around in the ramekin and dumping out any excess.) 2. Melt the chocolate and butter together, either in the microwave or in a double boiler. In a separate bowl, beat the eggs, egg yolks and sugar together until light and smooth. Add the vanilla extract. Whisk the chocolate mixture into the egg mixture. Stir in the flour and ground almonds. 3. Preheat the air fryer to 164°C. 4. Transfer the batter carefully to the buttered ramekins, filling halfway. Place two or three chocolate discs in the center of the batter and then fill the ramekins to ½-inch below the top with the remaining batter. Place the ramekins into the air fryer basket and air fry for 13 minutes. The sides of the cake should be set, but the centers should be slightly soft. Remove the ramekins from the air fryer and let the cakes sit for 5 minutes. (If you'd like the cake a little less molten, air fry for 14 minutes and let the cakes sit for 4 minutes.) 5. Run a butter knife around the edge of the ramekins and invert the cakes onto a plate. Lift the ramekin off the plate slowly and carefully so that the cake doesn't break. Dust with cocoa powder or icing sugar and serve with a scoop of ice cream and some coarsely chopped toasted almonds.

Apple Fries

Prep time: 10 minutes | Cook time: 7 minutes | Serves 8

Coconut, or avocado oil, for spraying
110 g plain flour
3 large eggs, beaten
100 g crushed digestive biscuits

55 g granulated sugar
1 teaspoon ground cinnamon
3 large Gala apples, peeled, cored and cut into wedges
240 ml caramel sauce, warmed

1. Preheat the air fryer to 192°C. Line the air fryer basket with baking paper and spray lightly with oil. 2. Place the flour and beaten eggs in separate bowls and set aside. In another bowl, mix together the crushed biscuits, sugar and cinnamon. 3. Working one at a time, coat the apple wedges in the flour, dip in the egg and then dredge in the biscuit mix until evenly coated. 4. Place the apples in the prepared basket, taking care not to overlap, and spray lightly with oil. You may need to work in batches, depending on the size of your air fryer. 5. Cook for 5 minutes, flip, spray with oil, and cook for another 2 minutes, or until crunchy and golden brown. 6. Drizzle the caramel sauce over the top and serve.

Pumpkin-Spice Bread Pudding

Prep time: 15 minutes | Cook time: 35 minutes | Serves 6

Bread Pudding:
175 ml heavy whipping cream
120 g canned pumpkin
80 ml whole milk
65 g granulated sugar
1 large egg plus 1 yolk
½ teaspoon pumpkin pie spice
⅛ teaspoon kosher, or coarse sea salt

1/3 loaf of day-old baguette or crusty country bread, cubed
4 tablespoons unsalted butter, melted
Sauce:
80 ml pure maple syrup
1 tablespoon unsalted butter
120 ml heavy whipping cream
½ teaspoon pure vanilla extract

1. For the bread pudding: In a medium bowl, combine the cream, pumpkin, milk, sugar, egg and yolk, pumpkin pie spice, and salt. Whisk until well combined. 2. In a large bowl, toss the bread cubes with the melted butter. Add the pumpkin mixture and gently toss until the ingredients are well combined. 3. Transfer the mixture to a baking pan. Place the pan in the air fryer basket. Set the fryer to 176°C cooking for 35 minutes, or until custard is set in the middle. 4. Meanwhile, for the sauce: In a small saucepan, combine the syrup and butter. Heat over medium heat, stirring, until the butter melts. Stir in the cream and simmer, stirring often, until the sauce has thickened, about 15 minutes. Stir in the vanilla. Remove the pudding from the air fryer. 5. Let the pudding stand for 10 minutes before serving with the warm sauce.

Pecan and Cherry Stuffed Apples

Prep time: 10 minutes | Cook time: 20 minutes | Serves 4

4 apples (about 565 g)	3 tablespoons brown sugar
40 g chopped pecans	¼ teaspoon allspice
50 g dried tart cherries	Pinch salt
1 tablespoon melted butter	Ice cream, for serving

1. Cut off top ½ inch from each apple; reserve tops. With a melon baller, core through stem ends without breaking through the bottom. (Do not trim bases.) 2. Preheat the air fryer to 176°C. Combine pecans, cherries, butter, brown sugar, allspice, and a pinch of salt. Stuff mixture into the hollow centers of the apples. Cover with apple tops. Put in the air fryer basket, using tongs. Air fry for 20 to 25 minutes, or just until tender. 3. Serve warm with ice cream.

Caramelized Fruit Skewers

Prep time: 10 minutes | Cook time: 3 to 5 minutes | Serves 4

2 peaches, peeled, pitted, and thickly sliced	½ teaspoon ground cinnamon
3 plums, halved and pitted	¼ teaspoon ground allspice
3 nectarines, halved and pitted	Pinch cayenne pepper
1 tablespoon honey	Special Equipment:
	8 metal skewers

1. Preheat the air fryer to 204°C. 2. Thread, alternating peaches, plums, and nectarines, onto the metal skewers that fit into the air fryer. 3. Thoroughly combine the honey, cinnamon, allspice, and cayenne in a small bowl. Brush the glaze generously over the fruit skewers. 4. Transfer the fruit skewers to the air fryer basket. You may need to cook in batches to avoid overcrowding. 5. Air fry for 3 to 5 minutes, or until the fruit is caramelized. 6. Remove from the basket and repeat with the remaining fruit skewers. 7. Let the fruit skewers rest for 5 minutes before serving.

Chocolate Chip Pecan Biscotti

Prep time: 15 minutes | Cook time: 20 to 22 minutes | Serves 10

135 g finely ground blanched almond flour	1 large egg, beaten
¾ teaspoon baking powder	1 teaspoon pure vanilla extract
½ teaspoon xanthan gum	50 g chopped pecans
¼ teaspoon sea salt	40 g organic chocolate chips,
3 tablespoons unsalted butter, at room temperature	Melted organic chocolate chips and chopped pecans, for topping (optional)
35 g powdered sweetener	

1. In a large bowl, combine the almond flour, baking powder, xanthan gum, and salt. 2. Line a cake pan that fits inside your air fryer with baking paper. 3. In the bowl of a stand mixer, beat together the butter and powdered sweetener. Add the beaten egg and vanilla and beat for about 3 minutes. 4. Add the almond flour mixture to the butter and egg mixture; beat until just combined. 5. Stir in the pecans and chocolate chips. 6. Transfer the dough to the prepared pan and press it into the bottom. 7. Set the air fryer to 164°C and bake for 12 minutes. Remove from the air fryer and let cool for 15 minutes. Using a sharp knife, cut the cookie into thin strips, then return the strips to the cake pan with the bottom sides facing up. 8. Set the air fryer to 148°C. Bake for 8 to 10 minutes. 9. Remove from the air fryer and let cool completely on a wire rack. If desired, dip one side of each biscotti piece into melted chocolate chips, and top with chopped pecans.

Chocolate Chip Cookie Cake

Prep time: 5 minutes | Cook time: 15 minutes | Serves 8

4 tablespoons salted butter, melted	110 g blanched finely ground almond flour
65 g granular brown sweetener	½ teaspoon baking powder
1 large egg	40 g low-carb chocolate chips
½ teaspoon vanilla extract	

1. In a large bowl, whisk together butter, sweetener, egg, and vanilla. Add flour and baking powder and stir until combined. 2. Fold in chocolate chips, then spoon batter into an ungreased round nonstick baking dish. 3. Place dish into air fryer basket. Adjust the temperature to 148°C and set the timer for 15 minutes. When edges are browned, cookie cake will be done. 4. Slice and serve warm.

Pumpkin Pudding with Vanilla Wafers

Prep time: 10 minutes | Cook time: 12 to 17 minutes | Serves 4

250 g canned no-salt-added pumpkin purée (not pumpkin pie filling)	1 tablespoon unsalted butter, melted
50 g packed brown sugar	1 teaspoon pure vanilla extract
3 tablespoons plain flour	4 low-fat vanilla, or plain wafers, crumbled
1 egg, whisked	Nonstick cooking spray
2 tablespoons milk	

1. Preheat the air fryer to 176°C. Coat a baking pan with nonstick cooking spray. Set aside. 2. Mix the pumpkin purée, brown sugar, flour, whisked egg, milk, melted butter, and vanilla in a medium bowl and whisk to combine. Transfer the mixture to the baking pan. 3. Place the baking pan in the air fryer basket and bake for 12 to 17 minutes until set. 4. Remove the pudding from the basket to a wire rack to cool. 5. Divide the pudding into four bowls and serve with the vanilla wafers sprinkled on top.

Brown Sugar Banana Bread

Prep time: 20 minutes | Cook time: 22 to 24 minutes

| Serves 4

195 g packed light brown sugar	1½ teaspoons baking powder
1 large egg, beaten	1 teaspoon ground cinnamon
2 tablespoons unsalted butter, melted	½ teaspoon salt
120 ml milk, whole or semi-skimmed	1 banana, mashed
250 g plain flour	1 to 2 tablespoons coconut, or avocado oil oil
	30 g icing sugar (optional)

1. In a large bowl, stir together the brown sugar, egg, melted butter, and milk. 2. In a medium bowl, whisk the flour, baking powder, cinnamon, and salt until blended. Add the flour mixture to the sugar mixture and stir just to blend. 3. Add the mashed banana and stir to combine. 4. Preheat the air fryer to 176ºC. Spritz 2 mini loaf pans with oil. 5. Evenly divide the batter between the prepared pans and place them in the air fryer basket. 6. Cook for 22 to 24 minutes, or until a knife inserted into the middle of the loaves comes out clean. 7. Dust the warm loaves with icing sugar (if using).

Kentucky Chocolate Nut Pie

Prep time: 20 minutes | Cook time: 25 minutes | Serves 8

2 large eggs, beaten	170 g milk chocolate chips
75 g unsalted butter, melted	2 tablespoons bourbon, or
200 g granulated sugar	peach juice
60 g plain flour	1 (9-inch) unbaked piecrust
190 g coarsely chopped pecans	

1. In a large bowl, stir together the eggs and melted butter. Add the sugar and flour and stir until combined. Stir in the pecans, chocolate chips, and bourbon until well mixed. 2. Using a fork, prick holes in the bottom and sides of the pie crust. Pour the pie filling into the crust. 3. Preheat the air fryer to 176ºC. 4. Cook for 25 minutes, or until a knife inserted into the middle of the pie comes out clean. Let set for 5 minutes before serving.

Crumbly Coconut-Pecan Cookies

Prep time: 10 minutes | Cook time: 25 minutes |

Serves 10

170 g coconut flour	125 g unsalted pecan nuts, roughly chopped
170 g extra-fine almond flour	150 g monk fruit, or equivalent sweetener
½ teaspoon baking powder	
⅓ teaspoon baking soda	¼ teaspoon freshly grated nutmeg
3 eggs plus an egg yolk, beaten	
175 ml coconut oil, at room temperature	⅓ teaspoon ground cloves

½ teaspoon pure vanilla extract	extract
½ teaspoon pure coconut	⅛ teaspoon fine sea salt

1. Preheat the air fryer to 188ºC. Line the air fryer basket with baking paper. 2. Mix the coconut flour, almond flour, baking powder, and baking soda in a large mixing bowl. 3. In another mixing bowl, stir together the eggs and coconut oil. Add the wet mixture to the dry mixture. 4. Mix in the remaining ingredients and stir until a soft dough forms. 5. Drop about 2 tablespoons of dough on the baking paper for each cookie and flatten each biscuit until it's 1 inch thick. 6. Bake for about 25 minutes until the cookies are golden and firm to the touch. Remove from the basket to a plate. Let the cookies cool to room temperature and serve.

Old-Fashioned Fudge Pie

Prep time: 15 minutes | Cook time: 25 to 30 minutes

| Serves 8

300 g granulated sugar	12 tablespoons unsalted butter, melted
40 g unsweetened cocoa powder	
70 g self-raising flour	1½ teaspoons vanilla extract
3 large eggs, unbeaten	1 (9-inch) unbaked piecrust
	30 g icing sugar (optional)

1. In a medium bowl, stir together the sugar, cocoa powder, and flour. Stir in the eggs and melted butter. Stir in the vanilla. 2. Preheat the air fryer to 176ºC. 3. Pour the chocolate filing into the crust. 4. Cook for 25 to 30 minutes, stirring every 10 minutes, until a knife inserted into the middle comes out clean. Let sit for 5 minutes before dusting with icing sugar (if using) to serve.

Protein Powder Doughnut Holes

Prep time: 25 minutes | Cook time: 6 minutes |

Makes 12 holes

50 g blanched finely ground almond flour	½ teaspoon baking powder
	1 large egg
60 g low-carb vanilla protein powder	5 tablespoons unsalted butter, melted
100 g granulated sweetener	½ teaspoon vanilla extract

1. Mix all ingredients in a large bowl. Place into the freezer for 20 minutes. 2. Wet your hands with water and roll the dough into twelve balls. 3. Cut a piece of baking paper to fit your air fryer basket. Working in batches as necessary, place doughnut holes into the air fryer basket on top of baking paper. 4. Adjust the temperature to 192ºC and air fry for 6 minutes. 5. Flip doughnut holes halfway through the cooking time. 6. Let cool completely before serving.

Strawberry Pastry Rolls

Prep time: 20 minutes | Cook time: 5 to 6 minutes per batch | Serves 4

85 g low-fat cream cheese
2 tablespoons plain yogurt
2 teaspoons granulated sugar
¼ teaspoon pure vanilla extract
225 g fresh strawberries

8 sheets filo pastry
Butter-flavored cooking spray
45-90 g dark chocolate chips (optional)

1. In a medium bowl, combine the cream cheese, yogurt, sugar, and vanilla. Beat with hand mixer at high speed until smooth (about 1 minute). 2. Wash strawberries and destem. Chop enough of them to measure 80 g. Stir into cheese mixture. 3. Preheat the air fryer to 164°C. 4. Filo pastry dries out quickly, so cover your stack of filo sheets with baking paper and then place a damp dish towel on top of that. Remove only one sheet at a time as you work. 5. To create one pastry roll, lay out a single sheet of filo. Spray lightly with butter-flavored spray, top with a second sheet of filo and spray the second sheet lightly. 6. Place a quarter of the filling (about 3 tablespoons) about ½ inch from the edge of one short side. Fold the end of the pastry over the filling and keep rolling a turn or two. Fold in both the left and right sides so that the edges meet in the middle of your roll. Then roll up completely. Spray outside of pastry roll with butter spray. 7. When you have 4 rolls, place them in the air fryer basket, seam side down, leaving some space in between each. Air fry for 5 to 6 minutes, until they turn a delicate golden brown. 8. Repeat step 7 for remaining rolls. 9. Allow pastries to cool to room temperature. 10. When ready to serve, slice the remaining strawberries. If desired, melt the chocolate chips in microwave or double boiler. Place 1 pastry on each dessert plate, and top with sliced strawberries. Drizzle melted chocolate over strawberries and onto plate.

Dark Chocolate Lava Cake

Prep time: 5 minutes | Cook time: 10 minutes | Serves 4

Olive oil cooking spray
30 g whole wheat flour
1 tablespoon unsweetened dark chocolate cocoa powder
⅛ teaspoon salt

½ teaspoon baking powder
60 ml raw honey
1 egg
2 tablespoons olive oil

1. Preheat the air fryer to 192°C. Lightly coat the insides of four ramekins with olive oil cooking spray. 2. In a medium bowl, combine the flour, cocoa powder, salt, baking powder, honey, egg, and olive oil. 3. Divide the batter evenly among the ramekins. 4. Place the filled ramekins inside the air fryer and bake for 10 minutes. 5. Remove the lava cakes from the air fryer and slide a knife around the outside edge of each cake. Turn each ramekin upside down on a saucer and serve.

Baked Peaches with Yogurt and Blueberries

Prep time: 10 minutes | Cook time: 7 to 11 minutes | Serves 6

3 peaches, peeled, halved, and pitted
2 tablespoons packed brown sugar

285 g plain Greek yogurt
¼ teaspoon ground cinnamon
1 teaspoon pure vanilla extract
190 g fresh blueberries

1. Preheat the air fryer to 192°C. 2. Arrange the peaches in the air fryer basket, cut side up. Top with a generous sprinkle of brown sugar. 3. Bake in the preheated air fryer for 7 to 11 minutes, or until the peaches are lightly browned and caramelized. 4. Meanwhile, whisk together the yogurt, cinnamon, and vanilla in a small bowl until smooth. 5. Remove the peaches from the basket to a plate. Serve topped with the yogurt mixture and fresh blueberries.

Hazelnut Butter Cookies

Prep time: 30 minutes | Cook time: 20 minutes | Serves 10

4 tablespoons liquid monk fruit, or agave syrup
65 g hazelnuts, ground
110 g unsalted butter, room temperature

190 g almond flour
110 g coconut flour
55 g granulated sweetener
2 teaspoons ground cinnamon

1. Firstly, cream liquid monk fruit with butter until the mixture becomes fluffy. Sift in both types of flour. 2. Now, stir in the hazelnuts. Now, knead the mixture to form a dough; place in the refrigerator for about 35 minutes. 3. To finish, shape the prepared dough into the bite-sized balls; arrange them on a baking dish; flatten the balls using the back of a spoon. 4. Mix granulated sweetener with ground cinnamon. Press your cookies in the cinnamon mixture until they are completely covered. 5. Bake the cookies for 20 minutes at 154°C. 6. Leave them to cool for about 10 minutes before transferring them to a wire rack. Bon appétit!

Pecan Bars

Prep time: 5 minutes | Cook time: 40 minutes | Serves 12

220 g coconut flour
5 tablespoons granulated sweetener
4 tablespoons coconut oil,

softened
60 ml heavy cream
1 egg, beaten
4 pecans, chopped

1. Mix coconut flour, sweetener, coconut oil, heavy cream, and egg. 2. Pour the batter in the air fryer basket and flatten well. 3. Top the mixture with pecans and cook the meal at 176°C for 40 minutes. 4. Cut the cooked meal into the bars.

Gluten-Free Spice Cookies

Prep time: 10 minutes | Cook time: 12 minutes | Serves 4

4 tablespoons unsalted butter, at room temperature

2 tablespoons agave nectar

1 large egg

2 tablespoons water

240 g almond flour

100 g granulated sugar

2 teaspoons ground ginger

1 teaspoon ground cinnamon

½ teaspoon freshly grated nutmeg

1 teaspoon baking soda

¼ teaspoon kosher, or coarse sea salt

1. Line the bottom of the air fryer basket with baking paper cut to fit. 2. In a large bowl, using a hand mixer, beat together the butter, agave, egg, and water on medium speed until light and fluffy. 3. Add the almond flour, sugar, ginger, cinnamon, nutmeg, baking soda, and salt. Beat on low speed until well combined. 4. Roll the dough into 2-tablespoon balls and arrange them on the baking paper in the basket. (They don't really spread too much but try to leave a little room between them.) Set the air fryer to 164°C, and cook for 12 minutes, or until the tops of cookies are lightly browned. 5. Transfer to a wire rack and let cool completely. Store in an airtight container for up to a week.

Chocolate Peppermint Cheesecake

Prep time: 5 minutes | Cook time: 18 minutes | Serves 6

Crust:

110 g butter, melted

55 g coconut flour

2 tablespoons granulated sweetener

Cooking spray

Topping:

110 g unsweetened cooking chocolate

180 g mascarpone cheese, at room temperature

1 teaspoon vanilla extract

2 drops peppermint extract

1. Preheat the air fryer to 176°C. Lightly coat a baking pan with cooking spray. 2. In a mixing bowl, whisk together the butter, flour, and sweetener until well combined. Transfer the mixture to the prepared baking pan. 3. Place the baking pan in the air fryer and bake for 18 minutes until a toothpick inserted in the center comes out clean. 4. Remove the crust from the air fryer to a wire rack to cool. 5. Once cooled completely, place it in the freezer for 20 minutes. 6. When ready, combine all the ingredients for the topping in a small bowl and stir to incorporate. 7. Spread this topping over the crust and let it sit for another 15 minutes in the freezer. 8. Serve chilled.

Appendix 1 Measurement Conversion Chart

MEASUREMENT CONVERSION CHART

VOLUME EQUIVALENTS(DRY)

US STANDARD	METRIC (APPROXIMATE)
1/8 teaspoon	0.5 mL
1/4 teaspoon	1 mL
1/2 teaspoon	2 mL
3/4 teaspoon	4 mL
1 teaspoon	5 mL
1 tablespoon	15 mL
1/4 cup	59 mL
1/2 cup	118 mL
3/4 cup	177 mL
1 cup	235 mL
2 cups	475 mL
3 cups	700 mL
4 cups	1 L

WEIGHT EQUIVALENTS

US STANDARD	METRIC (APPROXIMATE)
1 ounce	28 g
2 ounces	57 g
5 ounces	142 g
10 ounces	284 g
15 ounces	425 g
16 ounces (1 pound)	455 g
1.5 pounds	680 g
2 pounds	907 g

VOLUME EQUIVALENTS(LIQUID)

US STANDARD	US STANDARD (OUNCES)	METRIC (APPROXIMATE)
2 tablespoons	1 fl.oz.	30 mL
1/4 cup	2 fl.oz.	60 mL
1/2 cup	4 fl.oz.	120 mL
1 cup	8 fl.oz.	240 mL
1 1/2 cup	12 fl.oz.	355 mL
2 cups or 1 pint	16 fl.oz.	475 mL
4 cups or 1 quart	32 fl.oz.	1 L
1 gallon	128 fl.oz.	4 L

TEMPERATURES EQUIVALENTS

FAHRENHEIT(F)	CELSIUS(C) (APPROXIMATE)
225 °F	107 °C
250 °F	120 °C
275 °F	135 °C
300 °F	150 °C
325 °F	160 °C
350 °F	180 °C
375 °F	190 °C
400 °F	205 °C
425 °F	220 °C
450 °F	235 °C
475 °F	245 °C
500 °F	260 °C

Appendix 2 Air Fryer Cooking Chart

Air Fryer Cooking Chart

Beef

°C	Item	Temp (°F)	Time (mins)	Item	Temp (°F)	Time (mins)	°C
200	**Beef Eye Round Roast (4 lbs.)**	400 °F	45 to 55	**Meatballs (1-inch)**	370 °F	7	190
190	**Burger Patty (4 oz.)**	370 °F	16 to 20	**Meatballs (3-inch)**	380 °F	10	190
200	**Filet Mignon (8 oz.)**	400 °F	18	**Ribeye, bone-in (1-inch, 8 oz)**	400 °F	10 to 15	200
200	**Flank Steak (1.5 lbs.)**	400 °F	12	**Sirloin steaks (1-inch, 12 oz)**	400 °F	9 to 14	200
200	**Flank Steak (2 lbs.)**	400 °F	20 to 28				

Chicken

°C	Item	Temp (°F)	Time (mins)	Item	Temp (°F)	Time (mins)	°C
190	**Breasts, bone in (1 ¼ lb.)**	370 °F	25	**Legs, bone-in (1 ¾ lb.)**	380 °F	30	190
190	**Breasts, boneless (4 oz)**	380 °F	12	**Thighs, boneless (1 ½ lb.)**	380 °F	18 to 20	190
190	**Drumsticks (2 ½ lb.)**	370 °F	20	**Wings (2 lb.)**	400 °F	12	200
200	**Game Hen (halved 2 lb.)**	390 °F	20	**Whole Chicken**	360 °F	75	180
190	**Thighs, bone-in (2 lb.)**	380 °F	22	**Tenders**	360 °F	8 to 10	180

Pork & Lamb

°C	Item	Temp (°F)	Time (mins)	Item	Temp (°F)	Time (mins)	°C
200	**Bacon (regular)**	400 °F	5 to 7	**Pork Tenderloin**	370 °F	15	190
200	**Bacon (thick cut)**	400 °F	6 to 10	**Sausages**	380 °F	15	190
180	**Pork Loin (2 lb.)**	360 °F	55	**Lamb Loin Chops (1-inch thick)**	400 °F	8 to 12	200
200	**Pork Chops, bone in (1-inch, 6.5 oz)**	400 °F	12	**Rack of Lamb (1.5 – 2 lb.)**	380 °F	22	190

Fish & Seafood

°C	Item	Temp (°F)	Time (mins)	Item	Temp (°F)	Time (mins)	°C
200	**Calamari (8 oz)**	400 °F	4	**Tuna Steak**	400 °F	7 to 10	200
200	**Fish Fillet (1-inch, 8 oz)**	400 °F	10	**Scallops**	400 °F	5 to 7	200
190	**Salmon, fillet (6 oz)**	380 °F	12	**Shrimp**	400 °F	5	200
200	**Swordfish steak**	400 °F	10				

180 CHIPS 20 MINS

Printed in Great Britain
by Amazon

20034516R00038